Film Studies

Other books in this series by the same author

Film Studies

Andrew M. Butler

www.pocketessentials.com

This edition published in 2005 by Pocket Essentials
P.O.Box 394, Harpenden, Herts, AL5 1XJ
www.pocketessentials.com

Revised and reprinted 2008

A CIP catalogue record for this book is available from the British Library.

ISBN 978-1-904048-43-5

4 6 8 10 9 7 5

Typeset by Avocet Typeset, Chilton, Aylesbury, Bucks
Printed and bound in Great Britain by 4edge Limited, Essex

To Greg, Kathrina, Mark and Susan — in commemoration of nights at the Antelope; come join me in the Doves some time.

Acknowledgements

Eternal gratitude to the Prefab Four and to Becky, Ben, (new) Craig, Ed, George, Graham, Jo, Joel, Kenneth, Nathan, Neil, Ollie, Roxanne, Shaunagh, Tim and Tom for life-support beyond the call of duty. Thanks to all my colleagues, past and present, in the Department of Arts and Media at BCUC and the Department of Media at CCCU for their input into this book, knowingly or otherwise; the mistakes are, of course, all mine, especially the bit about dialectics. Thanks also to the many students whom I have taught and who have taught me film.

Greetings should go out to all the other people I've argued the toss about film with – Alex, Andrew, Bruce, Cathy, China, Dave, Estelle, Jack, Javier, Melissa, Mike, Richard, Robert, Sar, Sherryl, and Xav. See you in a multiplex or fleapit soon.

Contents

CONTENTS

Introduction

Once upon a time I discovered something about film: even the worst film has something to redeem it. That's not very profound, but it's kept me going.

After all, both times I saw *The Phantom Menace* on the big screen I didn't particularly like it, but the *Après Vu* was particularly fine the second time round. There's the acting, the themes, plot holes to drive a truck through and – always I felt the last refuge of the desperate – the cinematography. Long ago I fell in love with film, but also with talking and arguing about film.

This is a book to help you argue about film, and about different ways of understanding film: from the earliest thought about the medium and the nuts and bolts of how a film is put together, to approaches which focus on the directors, the stars, the nationality of the film or the genre, ways of understanding film from different critical approaches – Marxist, psychoanalytic, semiotic, feminist or queer. Clearly, there are overlaps between the ideas, and sometimes you will need to chase a theory from chapter to chapter. Sometimes you will find a certain amount of repetition.

Of course, this isn't the only book on how to understand film, but most of them rather assume that you're willing to suffer for your art and have submitted yourself to the four-hour Polish epics of the middle silent era. This book, on the other hand, assumes you have seen some of the more interesting films of recent years – *Reservoir Dogs* (1991), *Seven* (1995), *Pi* (1997) and *Fight Club* (1999) to name but four – and can understand and apply the concepts to them. Once we've seen the theories in action, then we might well get rather more out of those four-hour Polish epics of the middle silent era. Because if we don't see at least some black and white, silent or subtitled films, then we're missing out on a world of cinema.

In the second edition I managed to squeeze in a couple of additional chapters, and tidied a few things up elsewhere – and in the chapter on feminism I focused on a film directed by a woman rather than by a man (although, of course, a feminist reading does not just apply to films made by women). For this revision I have tinkered here and there, in some cases replacing old big names with new big names and bringing a number of details up to date. There are still things which have been forced out by space limitations.

Chapter 1

Some Early Film Theorists

In The Beginning ...

There was a moment in 1896 when the Russian Maxim Gorky described the experience of watching a film for the first time. It was a haunted world of soundless grey: a frozen picture of a train shuddering into life, complete with passengers and porters going about their voiceless lives. Fascinated though he was by it, Gorky could not see what purpose this new form had apart from being a money-making novelty. It was possible, he thought, that it may have some scientific purpose, for education, but it seemed all too likely that it was going to have something to do with sex.

Whilst Gorky's attendance at a film show was right at the dawn of cinema – Auguste Marie Louis Nicolas Lumière (1862–1954) and Louis Jean Lumière (1864–1948) patented a combined camera/projector in February 1895 and started showing short films in March – the medium had a long prehistory. Magic lanterns had been used for entertainment and education, but the fact that these were usually developed on glass plates limited the possibilities for a projection speed rapid enough to give the illusion of movement. Eadweard Muybridge had taken pictures of a horse in movement which could be strung together to show a brief sequence, and devices such as the zoetrope and the kinetoscope used principles akin to flicker books and optical illusions to show (but not project) movement. Thomas Edison, Louis Le Prince, William Friese Greene and Wordsworth Donisthorpe were among those trying to crack the problem – and Donisthorpe may have used a newly developed celluloid filmstock to film Trafalgar Square as early as 1890. According to Stephen Herbert, Donisthorpe, a libertarian, had anti-socialist views, and Trafalgar Square was a frequent point of civil protest; it is possible he wanted to use the film as part of a political lecture. It is clear that the technology of film was an idea whose time had come – what was less clear, for Gorky at least, was what it was for.

According to Tom Gunning, cinema up to about 1904 was a series of fairground attractions and spectacles: a man drinking a pint of beer, a wall being demolished and even Gorky's train arriving at a station. The films could be shown in reverse; a man spitting out a pint of beer, a wall being restored, a train reversing out of a station. On the one hand, film might be a depiction of reality – such as the films that Lumière made in the streets around their workshops. On the other, film might attempt to create its own reality, as seen in the trick films made by the French magician George Méliès. The distinction in film between art and reality – to some extent a false one – is a continuing thread in the debate about the nature and aesthetics of film as film.

12

Hugo Münsterberg (1863–1916)

Across in America, the Danzig-born Hugo Münsterberg was starting work as a professor at Harvard. His background was in psychology, with a particular interest in the perception of time and space, as well as reaction times and the concept of the persistence of vision. He had studied with a number of academics who were developing what became known as Gestalt psychology – the idea that the mind locates patterns in the colours, smells, tastes, sounds and feelings it perceives and organises the individual's sense of the world. Münsterberg's books on psychology made him one of the best-known academics in the United States, although his nationalistic support for German culture and his criticism of American society began to turn public opinion against him, especially after the outbreak of the First World War. So it was that, in 1914, he saw his first film, *Neptune's Daughter*.

Having previously thought that it was not fitting for a respected professor to indulge in such a common activity as going to the movies, he gave himself wholeheartedly to the phenomenon, interviewing industry figures, visiting film studios and even trying to make his own examples. The result of his researches was an article for *Cosmopolitan* and the book, *The Photoplay: A Psychological Study*, published just six months before he died in 1916. However, the book went out of print and was largely forgotten until 1970.

Münsterberg compared film to theatre, and noted that film stood at a greater distance from physical reality than a play did, and thus was closer to the mental processes of the individual. The drawbacks of early film

– lack of sound, lack of colour (aside from some tinting processes) – kept the depiction in a realm of fantasy rather than being accepted as real. The dumbshow performances meant that the essence of emotions had to be communicated without words to the audience.

He was also interested in the way that film could distort space and time. On the one hand, the medium was literally two-dimensional, with flat images projected onto a flat screen, but on the other there was an illusion of space. Not only that, but the film could take the viewer to a limitless number of locations. More importantly, flashbacks, flashforwards, dreams and memories could represent the non-linear nature of our thoughts. In Darren Aronofsky's *Pi* (1997) the main character Max's descent into mania and madness is depicted in camerawork, as we view the world from his point of view. The cutting between him and a subway passenger whose newspaper he had borrowed creates the paranoid illusion that Max is being followed, when in fact the two are simply walking in the same direction. Our consciousness to some extent begins and ends with Max's.

Münsterberg also applied his interest in optical illusions to film, in the problem of distinguishing foreground from background, especially when the only colours are black and white. Repeatedly in *Pi* there are shots of white square tiles, which are echoed in the white foreground squares of the Go board. Alternately, this might be perceived as a black grid pattern on a white background. Looking at images, the mind decides that part of it – squares or grid – is in the foreground and the rest is background – black or white surfaces. Once you perceive the illusion, you can decide which to watch.

Münsterberg, borrowing a term from the German psychologists Max Wertheimer and A. Korte, suggested that the brain has a phi-phenomenon, in which the mind controls what it perceives, and fills in the gaps between perceptions. The outside world is shaped by our perceptions of it. The stockmarket numbers shown in *Pi* appear to move along the display boards, when actually the lights stay still and just turn on and off in sequence. Just as music was the art form of the ear and painting the art form of the eye, so film was the art form of the mind. The right pictures could bring a sense of emotional and mental harmony to the minds of the contemporary audience, something desperately important to Münsterberg in the era of mass production, moral relativism and industrialised warfare.

Vsevolod Pudovkin (1893–1953)

Back in Russia, actor, writer and director Pudovkin combined the rôles of theorist and practitioner. Like Münsterberg, he drew on psychology, but in his case it was Russian. At the start of the twentieth century, Ivan Pavlov (1849–1936) had been experimenting with the idea of conditioning responses. In his classic experiment, Pavlov rang a bell whenever he fed a dog. The dog, associating the bell with food, would begin to salivate, even if food was not offered. Pudovkin reasoned that something similar would happen with human beings: if we perceive a particular gesture as associated with a given emotion, then the filmed gesture would indicate that emotion.

The rôle of the director was as a technician, who would guide the perception and response of a viewer through the linear structure of a film; the shift from, say, a long shot to a close up, was not something that jarred as other filmmakers feared, but represented the way that you suddenly focus on a detail in any situation. Of course Pudovkin assumes that audience reaction is predictable.

Pudovkin described a number of different editing techniques, which had different effects. Firstly, the impact of an image could be heightened by juxtaposing it with its opposite – poverty can be demonstrated in relation to wealth. In parallel editing, different events can be linked by a thread of continuity – perhaps best seen in the illusion of real time in the tv series *24*. Equally, an abstract theme or symbolism could link two elements – like the Kabbala and the stockmarket are by mathematics in *Pi*. Two narratives can be linked together by editing to make them appear simultaneous – such as showing both sides in a chase sequence. It's not that we see the different scenes simultaneously, but that we hold them in our minds simultaneously. Finally, there is editing which depends on a recurring visual leitmotif, an object, shape or style of lighting recurring through a film, such as the circles, squares and spirals of *Pi*.

The film is built frame by frame, shot by shot, scene by scene, sequence by sequence, as if the filmmaker is a bricklayer building a wall. The viewer's reactions are shaped and marshalled, with a slow increase of tension throughout the film's duration – the sensible director being careful not to exhaust the audience by peaking too early. It is in editing that the meaning of the film actually lies.

Sergei Eisenstein (1898–1948)

The filmmaker Sergei Eisenstein also felt the meaning of film lay in the editing, but sought discontinuity rather than continuity. He was influenced partly by the work of Lev Kuleshov (1899–1970), who had shown the same picture of a baby followed by a series of different images, discovering that the baby was perceived differently in each case. The meaning lay in the relation between the pictures rather than in the images themselves. Eisenstein exaggerated such contrasts with a technique known as dialectical montage.

He drew on the idea of dialectics as outlined by Georg Wilhelm Friedrich Hegel (1770–1831) and Karl Marx (1818–1883). For Hegel dialectics is the way that concepts or ideas develop, in the process shaping the world. A thesis produces an antithesis, and the conflict between the two is resolved in a new synthesis. For Marx, there is no synthesis – the conflict, being irreconcilable, produces a further antithesis. Marx suggests that the history of the world is a history of irreconcilable struggles between classes – master and slave in Greek, feudal and capitalist societies. Through continual revolution, a better society can be created.

As edited by Eisenstein, one image – one cell – is juxtaposed with another, and the conflict between the two produces an emotion, helping the viewer towards a revolutionary (ideally Marxist) consciousness. On the one hand, the impact of film was to be a fairground attraction, with the excitement of a roller coaster; on the other it was a revolution in intellect.

In one sequence of *Battleship Potemkin* (1925) soldiers march down the seemingly endless Odessa

Steps, massacring all that go before them. High angles are contrasted with low angles, close-ups with long shots, small objects with large, and so forth; sometimes we focus briefly on the fate of an individual, other times it is the mass of bodies that concerns us. After a while it becomes unclear where on the steps we are – near the top, near the bottom, halfway down the stairs … the helplessness and panic of the people on the steps and the power of the army is created by the contrasts in angles and heights of the camera work.

The techniques of montage have now been absorbed into Hollywood and other cinemas. One example is the tour of Washington DC in *Mr Smith Goes To Washington* (1939), which crossfades between locations and monuments, and signatures from the American Constitution. In a few minutes the viewer is given a potted military history of the United States from the War of Independence to the aftermath of the First World War, the musical accompaniment (including the British and American national anthems) adding to the emotions. Clearly Smith didn't go around Washington in chronological order, so an ideological or emotional reason must be sought for the choice to portray his tour in that order – a glorious past to be contrasted with a corrupt present, perhaps, but with the little boy and his grandfather at the Lincoln Memorial (for once not looking like a monkey) there is hope for the future.

The Capra-esque *The Hudsucker Proxy* (1994) has recourse to montage in its portrayal of the fall and rise of the hula-hoop – Norville Barnes's early demonstration of his invention gives way to a Kafka-esque sequence of accountants and designers, working on figures and stamping their approval. In silhouette we see the creative department devising names, whilst a secretary reads *War and Peace*; by the time they have decided she's well through *Anna Karenina*; meanwhile it is tested and manufactured and finally delivered to a shop. Cut to a toy shop window and the $3.99 price, soon slapped over with a lower price, a whole series of lower prices, then a sticker saying one is free with any purchase, and the disposal of the unwanted hoops. One hoop rolls across several streets to the feet of a waiting boy, who instinctively knows what to do, and then the kids want them, so the price goes back up.

Several months' of story time are compressed into a few minutes of screen time, as the narrative of the whole film is more concerned with his success or failure rather than the product itself. In the montage you lose sight of individual characters – we don't know the secretary, the creatives, the shopkeeper or any of the children by name, and Norville is sidelined as he anxiously watches the stock prices of Hudsucker Industries. The camera work draws attention to itself; when the hoop finds the kid, we move to an overhead shot, emphasising the move as the boy steps into the ring, the circle echoing Barnes's coffee ring on a newspaper, his hand-drawn design and even the clock at the top of the Hudsucker building.

Eisenstein argued that conflict is central to art in general and film in particular, because of its social mission, its nature and its methodology. Art should aim to expose and represent the complexities of the real world and to create correct political thinking in the viewer. There is then a conflict between the organic nature of the real world and the rational attempt to represent a portion of it. To maintain these contradictions, and to avoid too great an identification with the narrative, a dialectical style is necessary, with the relationship between two shots being more important than any single shot.

Whilst Eisenstein and Pudovkin disagreed on editing, they saw eye to eye on the coming of sound and the importance of unsynchronised sound, issuing a joint statement on the subject in 1928. Simply adding sound to pictures would lead to a greater sense of continuity between them (remember how music is used to link disparate locations in *Mr Smith Goes To Washington*), and thought may well give way to emotion and thus melodrama, especially with the introduction of theatrical-style dialogue. Whereas silent cinema was an international language (aside from intertitles), the introduction of sound would anchor each film in its native language. Instead, sound should be used to contrast with the images and add to the montage. Whilst their call went unheeded, there is no doubt that in the wake of synchronised sound, the expense of converting first studios and then cinemas to the new standard system allowed the bankers and the moneymen to begin to call the shots in the film industry. Whilst India now makes more films than any other country, English is the orthodox language of film.

Rudolf Arnheim (b.1904)

Arnheim, a film theorist, again from a psychological background, also distrusted synchronised sound. He argued that no one would expect a painting to have a soundtrack, and that the same should be expected of film. Dialogue paralyses action and prevents the essence of emotions being portrayed through posture and facial expressions. However, he sees no need for film to replicate the colour palette of nature, like realist painting, preferring the aesthetics of black, white and grey. Black shows up as a shape against a white background and vice versa – this is particularly true in the dark blacks and bright whites of *Pi*, which always threaten to flip into a negative image in the mind's eye.

Just as the lack of sound and colour from early film is seen as a positive aspect of film art, so the two-dimensionality of film is also crucial; this is another way of distinguishing the form from theatre. In theatre, there are hundreds of different vantage points from which to view the action, whereas in a film the director has chosen the viewpoint and places the camera in a given spot. Through careful choice of camera position, what is seen may be manipulated.

In his 1928 book, *Film As Art*, Arnheim exhaustively outlines the possibilities of film. For example, every object has to be photographed from a single angle, and objects are positioned in relation to others by perspective – closer objects appearing bigger, further smaller. The distance between the camera and the object can vary, as can the lighting and the apparent size. Through camera techniques such as editing, camera angles and lenses, the space–time continuum can be disrupted and the depth of field changed. Reality can apparently be reversed, speeded up or slowed down, and distorted through lenses, mirrors, multiple exposures or different levels of focus. Arnheim's concentration on film as an aesthetic, visual medium above anything else was taken up within the close analysis characteristic of *mise en scène* criticism, and it is this to which we will turn now.

Chapter 2

The Nuts And Bolts Of Film: Editing And *Mise En Scène*

In the early days of cinema, the camera was pointed and the film exposed. But it was quickly realised that rolls of film could be edited together to create a montage, the camera could move and what was being filmed could be controlled. Until the arrival of television, these capabilities distinguished cinema from the other arts.

The Long Take

To be perverse, let's begin by looking at films where there is little editing and the attempt to record a performance within a single shot. *Nanook Of The North* (1922) was praised for its use of long takes to faithfully record a fisherman waiting to catch something. This was considered more authentic than montage. Then there's Andy Warhol's *Empire*, a continuous take of the Empire State Building. Some people just have to make us suffer for their art.

On the other hand, there's no denying that the four-minute opening shot of *Touch Of Evil* (1958) is quality filmmaking, especially in the restored version. We see a bomb placed in the boot of a car on the Mexican/US border and follow various characters, including

Charlton Heston and Janet Leigh, through the border town and up to the border itself. This allows Welles – backed up by music – to draw the geography of the border for us, to show the culture, whilst we wait for the bomb to explode.

Alfred Hitchcock played with the long take in *Rope* (1948) and *Under Capricorn* (1949). In *Rope* two college students kill a friend and then have a dinner party around the box in which the body is hidden. Each take is approximately ten minutes long, the maximum amount of stock a camera could hold. Five of the ten edits in the film are masked by filling the screen with something black. There is a sense of claustrophobia and that these characters are being watched, and may be found out at any moment. All of this contributes to the suspense.

The single continuous take perhaps reaches its limit in Mike Figgis's *Timecode* (2000), in which four cameras record simultaneous events for about 90 minutes, culminating in an earthquake. All four films appear on screen at once. The form obscures the fact that it is second-rate material that is pure soap opera.

More recently, the unreliable World War II epic *Atonement* (2007) suddenly breaks into a long take following its characters around Dunkirk beach, with CGI assistance, which is surely cheating.

Camera Movements And Angles

The camera does not need to stay still; it can move forwards or backwards (track), from side to side (pan), or up and down (by tilting or a crane shot). The direction the camera is pointing distorts the image of what

23

is being filmed: looking down it can suggest an air of vulnerability or smallness, or looking upward, power and privilege. The camera can zoom in on an area or zoom out from it. It can look down from overhead and offer a bird's eye view. Such movements direct us to look in particular directions, reveal narrative points or try to generate a particular reaction – surprise, fear, suspense – within the audience. It can help or prevent us identifying with a character.

Most of the time the camera will be mounted on some kind of steady support, but the hand-held camera can be used to draw attention to events – for some reason this offers us the association of immediacy or prevents us from noting that they are staged. In contrast to the jerky, shaky movements of the hand-held camera, the Steadicam offers fluid movement – see *The Shining* (1980) where the camera could haunt the long corridors of the Overlook Hotel or the long opening shot (actually, several) of *Halloween* (1978).

Continuity Editing

Whilst in dialectical montage, as discussed in Chapter 1, the camerawork draws attention to itself, foregrounding the staging of events, the majority of films from Hollywood and mainstream narrative cinemas use what is known as continuity editing – when this works you barely notice the shift from shot to shot. Taken together, all the shots in a sequence give the impression of a continuous space. A sequence will typically begin with a shot which establishes a location for the characters, before focusing upon one or more of them and their actions. A number of factors contribute to the continuity: shot/reverse shot, the 180° Rule and the 30° Rule.

Shot/Reverse Shot

Perhaps the commonest editing technique is for the camera to focus upon a face, either head-on or to one side, and then to cut to either what they can see or to a shot peering over their shoulder. In dialogue sequences, what they are looking at is another character, so a piece of dialogue is followed by the reaction of the other character. The eye lines and camera angles are set up in such a way that the two characters are situated in relation to each other in a defined space, and the audience knows whether or not they are looking at each other. This general technique is known as shot/reverse shot or shot/counter-shot.

Typically this technique aids the audience in identifying with a particular character; entire sequences of *Vertigo* (1958) feature Scottie (James Stewart) tailing Madeleine (Kim Novak) in his car, alternating with the view of Madeleine driving or walking ahead of him. We barely notice that what Scottie sees is filmed on location in San Francisco, and that the shots of Scottie in the driving seat are done in the studio, with back projection standing in for the city. The editing creates a continuity for locations filmed on different days, and miles apart. The room that leads from an alley to a mall could be a studio set rather than a real place and this in turn need have no physical connection with the florist's shop he ends up spying on.

The 180° Rule

One means of enabling the viewer to maintain a sense of continuous space within a location is to avoid any shots that might apparently reverse the posture of the characters. This is achieved by imagining a line running across the set or location, over which the camera cannot cross; this is known as the 180° Rule. In any one set-up the camera can show Jimmy Stewart's face, and then the next shot could be anywhere to his right or even directly behind him. If the imaginary line is established on an axis from directly in front to directly behind, and we see a shot of his right profile, we cannot then cut to a shot from his left profile without getting confused about the space.

One example of this at work is the climax in *Seven* (1995) where the characters drive into the desert to locate the next body. An aerial view from a helicopter establishes the location before we move to inside the car: Detective Somerset drives, with the murderer John Doe caged at the back of the car; in some shots we see Somerset in profile. Perhaps stretching a point we sometimes see what Somerset sees in his rear-view mirror, although this matches up with the various angles of the back seat. The imaginary line can be drawn lengthways through the car with the action happening on the driver's side of the car. After more helicopter shots, we shift to the passenger's side of the car and Somerset's partner Mills's conversation with Doe. It appears that the imaginary line has moved because shots of what Doe sees predominate; we shift to the other side of the bars and it looks as if Mills is imprisoned. Before the car arrives at its destination the 180° rule is broken – the camera can point in any direction within the car. By now we've been educated as to the nature of the space within the car but at the same time we seem to be invited into Doe's space, and see what he sees – and we are being disconcerted.

The 30° Rule And The Jump Cut

Just as too great a leap between camera set-ups can confuse the audience, so too small a shift in angle can fail to feel like a cut at all. In fact, if there is any difference in angles of less than 30° then we may feel that it is a mistake, a break in the film rather than an edit. The practice of ensuring that there is a sufficient difference is known as the 30° Rule. To maintain a continuous space, the camera is limited as to where its next shot can come from.

At the same time, the queasiness felt by an audience at the breaking of the 30° Rule can be exploited by a canny director in the form of the jump cut. In Jean-Luc Godard's *A Bout De Souffle* (1959), Jean Seberg's character is driven around the streets of Paris by Jean-Paul Belmondo, who is holding forth about women. The audience appears to be staring down the back of her neck as the background of streets continually cuts. There's a new edginess to the film.

The jump cut even shows up in Steven Spielberg's *Jaws* (1975), when Roy Scheider's character is on the beach, looking out for the shark he believes is still out there in the bay. A group of pleasure seekers walks by, and we are suddenly closer to him. The trick is repeated. More recently, Bill Bennett's road movie *Kiss Or Kill* (1997), in which both of the protagonists think their partner is guilty of a string of brutal murders, is made more paranoiac by its use of jump cuts. Because we are aware we haven't seen everything, we begin to imagine what we might have missed.

Having considered some basic ways of putting different shots together, it is now necessary to look at what is within the shot: the fictional world of the film, or diegesis. Taken together the visual elements on the screen − setting, lighting, symbols, motifs and so on − form the *mise en scène*, a term taken from stage drama. This became central to the analysis of the *Cahiers Du Cinéma* critics in the 1950s and afterwards, as a means of distinguishing film criticism from that of other media, as well as being the element which was most controlled by the director. I'm going to consider these elements in relation to *The Usual Suspects* (1995).

Setting

The earliest films were made in and around the engineers' workshops. In time, though, the control necessary over a particular environment to make a successful film meant that sets were being used, especially for interior shots where a studio afforded more space to fit the camera, crew and lighting equipment.

No matter how fine the set, there is a difference in feel between studio and location footage − the dynamism of characters driving real cars through real streets in *Touch Of Evil* is very different from the reshoots done in front of back projection. This is not to hold out a demand for the realism of a set, simply to note a difference. The painted boat at the end of the street in *Marnie* (1964) is clearly a painting, but this only serves to draw attention to it being there. But whether it is studio or location, the setting contributes to the meaning of the film.

Consider the first two times the five criminals are brought together in *The Usual Suspects* (1995), the line-up and the holding cell. The first is familiar, although we are more often situated on the other side of the glass, trying to identify the culprit. The flat white wall with the black lines is a useful foil against which to establish the characters, little distracts us and we can compare them. The cell to which the characters are moved is dingier, clearly not for public view, with a green/brown shade to the wall. There are windows in the back wall, albeit a series of small ones in rows, but it is not clear whether this backs onto a corridor or the outside world. These two scenes and settings enclose the five together and unveil the tensions between them, in contrast to the earlier scenes of the individuals in isolation.

Lighting

In lighting, a number of factors need examining: type, source, quality and colour. The light from a candle should be different from that of a bulb or that of the sun. By source I mean the point of origin and the direction of its beams. This can be naturalistic, i.e. from a direction that we would expect light to be coming from in a given scene, or it can be expressionist and have some kind of symbolic meaning. (For financial and then aesthetic reasons *Das Kabinett Des Dr Caligari* (1919) had many of its shadows painted directly onto the sets.) The quality includes the light's brightness and continuity – it might be diffuse, it might be cutting through fog or smoke and it might be flickering. Finally the colour of the light – red, green, blue and so forth – will have an impact on how we relate to a scene.

Objects appear differently according to how they are lit. A light in front will highlight them, whereas one from behind will create a silhouette. Side lighting, lighting from below or lighting from above will all cast different forms of shadows, and generate different moods. In Classical Hollywood a three-point lighting scheme was developed: a fill light placed next to the camera pointed towards the character to keep shadows to a minimum; a key light diagonally across the character was the most important illumination; and a back light emphasised the character.

In *The Usual Suspects*' line-up, the light is bright and white, so Keaton has to shade his eyes, whereas in the cell it tends towards the muddy and green, although as the scene progresses and the characters talk about getting together for a job, it begins to be more blue. In the various interrogation scenes the characters seem to be lit from above to make it clear who is being interrogated.

Acting

Styles of acting have varied over the last century, from the stylised overacting of the silent era to actors like Cary Grant seeming to act like themselves. Delivery of dialogue, body language and movement can all add meaning to a performance; for example, the overlapping dialogue of screwball comedy in a film like *Bringing Up Baby* (1938) is quite different from the always distinct dialogue in a Hal Hartley film. The method acting school has produced some great performances over the last 50 years, notably from Robert de Niro, but sometimes the actor seems to be reduced to mumbling; it can become mannered rather than real. Different styles of acting within a film can lead to an unevenness in the final product.

Verbal, introduced by his feet in *The Usual Suspects*, seems very self-contained, his right hand hooked around his left arm as he shuffles in, and this can be contrasted with Fenster's stressed pacing in the cell. Fenster's dialogue is virtually impossible to decode at times, a fact the film points out on a number of occasions. Hockney, in contrast, is lying down on a bench, propped up by his elbows, waiting for the events to run their course, almost resigned, and McManus is sitting down. Keaton, when he comes in and sits away from the others, is more deflated or defeated. He sits huddled inside the jacket which he had carried into the line-up.

Costume, Make-Up And Props

Clearly, each of the characters has their own costume, which acts as a pointer to their personality or style. Keaton, the upcoming businessman, has a brown/cream suit and a light blue shirt, respectable but relaxed. Fenster's shirt is bright red with a wide collar and undone buttons, under a black jacket; it is extravagant and outgoing whilst attempting to be stylish. Hockney is wearing a vest and a bomber jacket, and McManus a dark polo neck T-shirt and a long leather jacket, usually a sign of a rebellious or unpredictable streak. (Compare the costume contrasts in *Seven*, where the methodical Somerset wears a tie, shirt, waistcoat and sober suit and the inexperienced and potentially maverick Mills's tie is never done up; again a leather jacket is worn.) Verbal is the scruffiest of the five, cardigan over the top of a shirt which is not tucked fully into his trousers, and a T-shirt worn under that. He is clearly someone whom fashion has left behind.

Make-up isn't noticeable on any of the five, although Fenster's hair is clearly treated in some way. Make-up, like continuity camerawork, is usually invisible – several of the corpses in *Seven* presumably 'wear' make-up, but we don't notice it. In horror films make-up is a way of suggesting who is dead and who is alive, and of providing shocks. In German Expressionism, make-up is part of the aesthetics of the film.

Props may be considered as an extension of costume because they tend to be associated with a particular character. In this case, Keaton's jacket is drawn attention to, although you wouldn't normally think of it as a prop. The general rule is that if attention is drawn to any prop early on in the film – say, a cigarette lighter, a gun in a drawer, anti-gravity boots – it will assume major importance in the last part of the film. In the two scenes discussed, the only real prop is the card they read their line off in the line-up – but cigarette lighters do assume significance on the plot at various points.

Symbols And Motifs

Sometimes elements of the *mise en scène* seem to take on greater importance than their rôle within a particular scene – an object, a shape, a colour will appear in several scenes and have some sense of significance about it. The colour red seems to be a common recurring motif – in the dress of Natalie Wood and then the coat of James Dean in *Rebel Without A Cause* (1955), in the eponymous Marnie's panic attacks, in the strange scuttling dwarf in *Don't Look Now* (1973) and the small girl in the camp in *Schindler's List* (1993). Red can mean anger, blood, passion, hate, heat, and no doubt many other things. In Peter Greenaway's *The Cook, The Thief, His Wife And Her Lover* (1989) there are four distinct zones – the blue of the outside, the green of the kitchen, the red of the restaurant and the white of the toilets. Dresses, scarves and sashes change colour between areas, even when the camera has appeared to pan in time to the characters moving between rooms. The connotations of the colours draw attention to the different functions of the zones in relation to food and sex.

I've already noted the feet of Verbal at the start of the line-up and at the end of the film, but this also echoes the feet of the barely seen Keyzer Soze on the boat. The lighting of cigarettes – by Keyzer, Keaton and Verbal – and the starting of fires are related, along with the fiery hell which Soze's family has experienced.

Of course, there is much more that can be said about the *mise en scène*, its meaning and the way its elements interact. In addition, there are different camera angles – the fish-eye lens, bullet-time, track/reverse zoom – and ways of cutting in cinema. Film Studies has emphasised those directors who control what is in the frame and this is central to the *auteur* theory discussed in the next chapter.

Chapter 3

Auteur Theories

French Origins: The Policy Of *Auteurs*

The *auteur* theory put the idea of *mise en scène* on the Film Studies map, and has its origin in the writings of a group of young critics working for the French film journal *Cahiers Du Cinéma*. A key article is François Truffaut's 'A Certain Tendency In French Cinema' (1954). He objected to the stifling psychological realism typical of French cinema in the post-war period, and how notions of what a French film should be – primarily a literary adaptation – limited its scope. Truffaut claimed that writers within the French cinema thought that the most important part of the film was the words, and that the director just added some pictures. The scriptwriters considered their work to be demeaning, and often tried to appeal to the lowest common denominator in their audience. In contrast, Truffaut praised films where the director had contributed to the script and where something truly cinematic was taking place. Primarily this meant the look of the film, its *mise en scène*, and the responsibility for this could be traced to the director.

The *Cahiers* critics were looking across the Atlantic to the industrial practices developed in Hollywood and to directors such as Alfred Hitchcock and Howard Hawks. An *auteur* was a person, usually a director, who was able to stamp his own identity upon a film despite the commercial pressures within the studio system – compare the way that aspects of David Fincher's vision can be traced in *Alien³* (1992), despite the pressures from the studio for a product that would draw in and expand upon audiences for *Alien* (1979) and *Aliens* (1986). The *auteur* is to be contrasted with the *metteur en scène*, the director for hire who was thought by the *Cahiers* critics to be an artisan rather than an artist.

The visual style of a given film – the underlighting of David Fincher's films, the rotating fans of Ridley Scott's, the deep focus of Orson Welles's – is an indication of the work of an individual practitioner or the recognisable signature of a given director. The *Cahiers* critics placed less emphasis upon the recognition of certain recurring themes – the wrong man in Hitchcock's films, say – although this was also a factor in some of their analysis. Such close analysis of a film formed a *politique des auteurs*, a policy for/of authors.

Andrew Sarris: The *Auteur* Theory

The American critic Andrew Sarris created a theory of the *auteur*. In his essay 'Notes On The *Auteur* Theory, 1962', he attempts to redeem Hollywood cinema as worthy of study instead of European art cinema – artists were at work within the studio system. The production line of Hollywood offers opportunities for the identification of themes, structures, narratives and aesthetics in films that in turn show the personality of the director.

Sarris argued that Hollywood cinema was as good as

– if not better – than European cinema, and the identification of *auteurs* was a way of demonstrating what was great about it. Further, the history of these *auteurs* was also the history of Hollywood. Good films were made by good directors – bad films by bad directors. Of course, every director can have an off day, and lousy directors have made the odd decent movie (say, Spielberg up to about *Jaws* (1975)), but predominantly *auteurs* make the better films. Sarris isolates three areas of competence – technique, personal style and inner meaning – and links these to directors as technician, stylist and *auteur*. It is possible for a *metteur en scène* to improve and become an *auteur*, or for an *auteur* to become a *metteur en scène*. The canon of *auteurs* is one of shifting reputations.

The problem with his approach is that, short of interviewing the director about every tiny or major choice taken during shooting, the critic risks identifying a recurring motif as a deliberate decision made by this individual director, rather than a decision that could have been made by any director. In Fincher's *Seven* (1995), *The Game* (1997) and *Fight Club* (1999) there are three central characters, two male, one female – but the same could be said of Andrew Niccol's film *Gattaca* (1997). How can we be sure we're dealing with Fincher rather than Niccol, or finding a pattern where there is none?

We need to go further. We can identify a director who likes the romantic triangle of two men and a woman (made complicated by the genetics in *Alien³*), a murky, underlit *mise en scène*, depressing endings (the death of Ripley in *Alien³*, the murderous climax of *Seven*, the suicide within a game of *The Game*, the fall of the towers in *Fight Club*), protagonists who aren't in control of their destinies (Ripley thanks to infection by alien DNA and the Company, Mills as manipulated by John Doe, Nicholas Van Orton at the mercy of his brother Conrad, the narrator who doesn't realise he is Tyler Durden), and the killing of characters we care for (Newt and t'other chap during the opening credits, thus negating the last half hour of *Aliens*, Tracey in *Seven*, Meat Loaf in *Fight Club* … [OK, so this is one argument I'll lose]). The more aspects we can identify, the more precisely we can locate an *auteur*.

Peter Wollen: *Auteur* Structuralism

In his book *Signs And Meaning In The Cinema* (1969), the British critic Peter Wollen formalises this position of the identity of a director being constructed by the viewer, by applying structuralist or semiotic theory. This is a topic to which we will return in Chapter 5. Wollen points out that the impact of American cinema on post-war France was exaggerated because it was so much a breath of fresh air after the limitations of the wartime repertoire, plus the economics of the Paris cinema clubs exposed the French cinephiles to many more films than would have usually been the case. Authorship in this context risks becoming a cult of personality, with certain directors burning very brightly. He also criticises Sarris' position for its over-unification of the *Cahiers* approach, which, after all, had been evolved by individuals rather than codified by manifestos: some of the *Cahiers* critics actually preferred *metteurs en scène* to *auteurs*, and some were more interested in theme than style. Directors of the second rank were acclaimed before any real sense of their worth could be arrived at – and now, with almost every movie being labelled 'An [insert director's name here] Film' the currency is devalued. Is Kevin Smith any less worthy of attention because he doesn't label his films in the same way as Ridley Scott or Michael Mann, or, to choose less stylish examples, Joe Johnstone or Chris Columbus?

Wollen argues for an analysis of directors who have had lengthy careers – in particular Howard Hawks and John Ford. Steven Spielberg or Woody Allen might be considered as *auteurs* after three decades, but it is simply too early to tell for, say, Kevin Smith or Spike Lee. A director who keeps on making the same film (the relationship between a sensitive young man and his girlfriend, threatened by his foul-mouthed best friend in contemporary New Jersey) may be impressive, but is not great in Wollen's model. On the other hand, a director may be an *auteur* even if he has made a film about people being menaced by a truck or a shark, visits from aliens of various kinds, slaves who go home, Jews that survive the holocaust or a completely misconceived sequel to *Peter Pan*.

Wollen writes of locating 'antinomies' within the movies of individual directors. These are opposing sets of ideas, such as culture vs nature and civilised vs savage. It is not that one set of characters represents one side of the oppositions – the good guys having the characteristics which society accepts, the bad guys having those that society disapproves of – but that these oppositions shift and unsettle. It is easiest to see this at work in Westerns, where it is tempting simply to assume that the cowboys are the white hats (or civilised) and the Indians the black (savage).

In *The Searchers* (1956) John Wayne's character Ethan Edwards is the hero who goes in search of his kidnapped niece. His quest invokes a whole series of oppositions: garden vs wilderness, settler vs nomad, civilised vs savage, European vs Indian and so forth. The quest shows Edwards cares for his family – and yet he has no real connection with it. It is so long since he has visited them that he mistakes the younger niece for the older. He comes in at the start of the film as a nomad visiting settlers, he spends five years in search of a lost settler and, having reunited the settlers, sets out again to be a nomad. Being of European origin, Edwards should be a civilised person, and yet he is outside the law, refusing to be cowed by the sheriff's orders; it is he who will decide whether his lost niece will live, not the Indians. Wollen traces such antinomies in a number of John Ford Westerns – *My Darling Clementine* (1946) and *The Man Who Shot Liberty Valance* (1962) among others – and these could be found in the much earlier *Stagecoach* (1939). According to Wollen, the relations between the two vary from film to film in Ford's oeuvre, whereas in Howard Hawks's, the oppositions are fairly constant. Variety and consistency become necessary for the *auteur* and become a yardstick for quality.

The relationships between antinomies can be traced in *Seven*: civilised vs savage, moral vs immoral, detective vs criminal, hunter vs hunted, virtue vs sin, married vs unmarried, books vs gun, sane vs insane and so on. The first three pairs should be a simple mapping of Somerset/Mills vs John Doe. After all, our two heroes are the gallant detectives trying to hunt down a savage serial killer. However, the film is careful to establish

Somerset's learning and appreciation of classical music (a taste shared by the security guards in the city library), whereas Mills is shown playing with his dogs for relaxation and needs a set of Cliff's Notes to understand the literary allusions which are second nature to John Doe. Mills is happy to break the law by kicking down a door to a flat that they don't have a warrant to enter, and even Somerset's use of the secret services to discover John Doe's whereabouts is on the edge of the law.

Further, John Doe's ability to locate Mills and his wife shows detecting skills – if only by finding the right person to bribe – and his calculated surrender to the police keeps him firmly in control. Doe's punishment of sin is complete with Mills embodying wrath – just as he recognises that his own sin is envy of Mills' lifestyle. But in his murder of Mills' wife, he has exhibited lust, and in his belief that he has the right to judge others, he is also prey to the sin which caused Lucifer to fall: pride. The punisher of sins is himself guilty of sins, and only Somerset is virtuous. And the only murder we actually see is Mills shooting Doe. The gun is associated with the detectives, rather than the criminal.

To move briefly through the other antinomies: Somerset is the kind of person he is because he didn't marry; Mills ended up mad because he did. Doe, we can safely assume from the lack of a paper trail, is a confirmed bachelor. Is Doe insane? Probably. But Mills is likely to be the one led off to psychiatric evaluation at the end of the film.

In a 1972 afterword to *Signs And Meaning*, Wollen argues against the use of the *auteur* theory to insert the idea of a personal vision within cinema and insists that the theory should not be a cult of personality that celebrates the unified artistic vision of an artist who just happens to be working in the medium of film. The name of the *auteur* is a convenient label under which we can trace a particular set of contesting ideas.

Some of the responsibility for the meaning of the film devolves to the viewer, who is actively reading the film. The film that they see is not necessarily the one made by the director – in the sense that the critic doesn't necessarily see the film the director has consciously decided to make from the material available. And it isn't necessarily the film seen by other critics. Whilst Wollen had identified certain recurrent structures within film, there is no universal structure of film within which these structures can in turn be fitted.

Equally, these structural relationships can be located in films by different directors. A particular set of characteristics – say, the combination of smooth tracking shots with shot/reverse-shot structures and even montage, the portrayal of alienated individuals in a hostile environment, the preoccupation with looking and psychological states of mind, the importance of female characters, and the killer as gay – could be identified as Hitchcockian, irrespective of Alfred's intentions in making a movie. At the same time, if we were to pick a Brian De Palma film at random – say, *Carrie* (1976) – we may well recognise many of the same codes. Is this an act of homage on De Palma's part – which would involve researching his public pronouncements about his influences – or is it that there is no problem in locating the Hitchcockian in De Palma?

ANDREW M. BUTLER

Auteurs Outside Hollywood

The focus of *auteur* criticism has been on directors
working within a classical Hollywood system –
Hitchcock, Ford, Hawks, even Welles – because these
were seen as mavericks with a vision within a system.
As a lecture sequence in the Australian film *Love And
Other Catastrophes* (1996) points out, cases could be
made for Woody Allen, Spike Lee and Quentin
Tarantino. The emergence of independent film in the
1980s and 1990s – with Lee and directors like Jim
Jarmusch, Hal Hartley and Kevin Smith – has led to a
cinema focused upon individual charismatic figures
who have personal visions they wish to express, and
who act as one-person publicity machines. Personal
projects drive these people rather than the wish to be
hired within Hollywood. In addition, if we follow
Wollen, for many of these it is just too early to tell if
they are *auteurs*. (OK – sidebar. How come Jean Vigo
got to be an *auteur* having made fewer than two
movies? What kind of lengthy career is that?)

Thus far I've discussed the *auteur* theory and
Hollywood product, with independent filmmakers
influenced by Hollywood or with independent filmmakers who end up being financed by Hollywood
studios, even if they have been given the sense of
creative freedom. But what about *auteurs* in the rest of
the world? A case can be made for *auteurs* in European
cinema, and by implication other cinemas, although the
economic conditions downplay the sense of an *auteur*
whose material is shaped in a battle with a money-
making studio.

Pedro Almodóvar has recurring themes of gender

42

relations, fluid sexuality and the ambiguous morality of authority, and a recognisable *mise en scène*, involving kitsch, stylisation and bright colours. As writer and director he maintains much control over his films, and his use of his brother Augustin as producer presumably adds to this. In his early films Almodóvar frequently cast Carmen Maura and Antonio Banderas, although the rôles that Banderas played as murderous fan in *La Ley Del Deseo* (*Law Of Desire*, 1987) and as sadistic kidnapper in *¡Átame! (Tie Me Up! Tie Me Down!*, 1989) were quite different from the shy son that he played in *Mujeres Al Borde De Un Ataque De Nervios* (*Women On The Verge Of A Nervous Breakdown*, 1988). Carmen Maura also played a variety of rôles rather than a fixed archetype. Later on, Almodóvar cast Victoria Abril and then Penélope Cruz, in parallel to the way Hitchcock cast Grace Kelly and Tippi Hedren or Cary Grant and James Stewart in his films. In *Volver* (2006) both Cruz and Maura appeared together, but playing different generations of the same family and thus fulfilling different functions in the narrative.

Questioning The Auteur Theory

Are the Maura films by Almodóvar different to the Abril ones? Can we distinguish between a Grant/ Hitchcock film and a Stewart one — for that matter how does a Hitchcock/Grant movie differ from a Hawks/Grant one? To what extent is the director a unified source of meaning?

Whether the *auteur* theory is one that suggests the director has a vision, or whether the marks of authorship lead us to posit a 'Hitchcock' or a 'Fincher', the emphasis in this kind of criticism is placed on the director. This neglects the contribution made to the *mise en scène* by the director of photography or even the set designer, and ignores the rôle of the writer, the interference of producers, and the performances of the stars. And most audiences will go to see a Johnny Depp or (apparently) a Keira Knightley movie movie rather than a Paul McGuigan movie. Most moviegoers probably couldn't tell you who directed the film they have just seen.

Chapter 4

Marxism

Karl Marx (1818–1883)

Karl Marx is probably the most influential thinker of the last two centuries, both on those who accepted his ideas and, oddly, on those who rejected them. Born into a comfortable middle-class family in Germany, he studied law at the University of Bonn where he was distracted by drinking, duelling and writing love poems. He moved to Berlin in 1836 and was influenced by Hegel's ideas about dialectics. Marx began to use Hegel's ideas to critique religion, as well as the political and economic state of Germany, and he moved into political journalism. In 1843 Marx emigrated to Paris, where he met workers in Paris and then his lifelong collaborator, Frederick Engels (1820–1895), the son of a Manchester businessman. Marx and Engels started to write together, Engels helping out when Marx got writer's block. On a visit to London he was commissioned, with Engels, to write the manifesto for the Communist Party. They completed this in 1848, a year of revolutions across Europe. The next year, having been expelled from several countries, Marx moved to London where he was to continue writing – and calling for revolution – until his death. Marx and Engels said little about film as they died before its prominence – however, their ideas can still be applied to the medium. In particular Marxist critics are interested in the material, economic and ideological contexts in which films are made and viewed.

The Background To Marxism

To understand Marxism, you need to understand its background in the ideas of the Enlightenment, Parisian class struggles and British utopian socialism.

The period of the Enlightenment – the eighteenth century – saw the emergence of a series of thinkers who wanted to use logic and science to understand the world and to put humanity firmly in charge. Writers, scientists and satirists such as François Voltaire (1694–1778), Denis Diderot (1713–1784), Gotthold Lessing (1729–1781) and Immanuel Kant (1724–1804) argued that the universe has a material rather than a spiritual origin, and can be understood by the application of intellect. The intellect can set the individual free, an individual is a citizen of the world and has certain rights (and responsibilities). These ideas helped to pave the way for the written constitutions for the new republics of the United States (1776) and France (1789), in the case of the former ensuring the separation of state from any religion. The individual had the right to be educated – the following century saw a huge growth in demands for and provision of education for the masses – and the right to vote – even, eventually, the right for women to vote – in a democratic state. The Industrial Revolution, which also began in the eighteenth century, saw humanity harnessing the elements, and the rise of mass production and, in time, mass reproduction, mass media and mass communication. Hegel argued that the basis of humanity is mental not spiritual, and that the history of ideas is the history of contradictions and counter-positions. You get a basic idea which comes into conflict with its opposite, and the original idea is therefore modified: thesis – antithesis – synthesis. Of course, it does not stop at synthesis, but moves on to a new antithesis. This idea is known as dialectics, and Marx's application and modification of the idea to the way the real, material, solid world operates is known as dialectical materialism.

From Marx's knowledge of contemporary and historical France, he knew that there was an ongoing dialectical struggle between two different classes, whether it was the lord and serf in the feudal days, or capitalist and worker in his own time. Each time the battle would lead to mutual destruction or a revolution in society. In his day, workers were treated like cogs in machinery, to be exploited to make money for capitalists and thrown away when no longer needed. The capitalist might risk his or her investment – but the long shifts of the worker literally risked life and limb. The worker was alienated from his or her labour.

A number of socialists had suggested possibilities for change – including Henri Saint-Simon (1760–1825), Robert Owen (1771–1858) and Charles Fourier (1772–1837). For example, Owen had set up a community in New Lanark, Scotland, with better housing, a school, a co-operative shop and a sense of community involvement in the factory. Whilst this form of caring capitalism was better than the standard model, and might slowly improve conditions more generally, it was simply a sticking plaster. Marx wanted radical change for the better rather than gradualism.

Base And Superstructure

Central to Marx's ideas are the ideas of base and superstructure. The former is the way that the economics of a given society are organised, for example whether it is an agricultural or industrial economy, who owns and exploits the resources and what form of economic exchange takes place. The base determines the superstructure – which consists of law, politics, religion, education, family structures, art, culture and media. A particular kind of culture arises within given economic conditions. As those conditions change, so does the superstructure.

This model should not be viewed too rigidly. There may be some lag in change as older forms of culture cling on. The different elements of the superstructure interrelate. For example, the political landscape can affect the funding, distribution and certifying of films – the banning of so-called video nasties in the early 1980s was a political act. Further, elements of the superstructure can have an impact upon the base – as in the British government's actions against the mining and other major industries in the 1980s and the privatisation of public utilities.

Nevertheless, a film needs to be considered as a product of a particular time in a period of historical development, and is produced under certain economic conditions. It reflects and comments upon class relations within its originating community, even on occasions criticising such structures. The bottom line is that a film is a means of selling tickets – as well as iced drinks, peanuts, popcorn, ice cream and nachos – by appealing to as wide an audience as possible. The bigger the budget, the less likely it is to be difficult or challenging.

Amy Heckerling's *Clueless* (1995) is a teen rewriting of Jane Austen's *Emma*, set in the Los Angeles area. Cher Horowitz's father is a lawyer who charges $500 an hour, and spoils her rotten. She has wardrobes full of the latest clothes, racks of shoes and her own mobile phone. Defined by her possessions, she rules the roost at her school and gets to decide who is in and who is out, as well as matchmaking teachers and pupils alike. She is part of the bourgeois class, with little sympathy for the people her family employs.

The film was made under the aegis of Paramount Studios, which can be traced back to Adolph Zukor's founding of the Famous Players Film Corp in 1912. After several changes of name, and a bankruptcy in 1935, the company was bought by Gulf + Western in 1966; in 1989 they renamed themselves Paramount Corporation. In 1994, the year before the release of *Clueless*, the Paramount Corporation was bought by Viacom, itself a descendent offshoot of CBS, a company which it then merged with in 1999. This interconnection of ownership allows a little cross-promotion, as key scenes of Cher getting to know future boyfriend Josh involve them watching *Beavis And Butthead* and *Ren And Stimpy*, both products of MTV, a Viacom tv station. On the other hand, the soundtrack album, another means of exploiting the film, was contracted out to Capitol Records, a subdivision of EMI.

Ideology

Any economic system seeks to perpetuate itself, and power-holders seek to make us share their ways of thinking – including the idea that it is fitting that they be in charge. Ideology is a set of (mis)representations of the world that make us see it in a particular way, and films might be seen as little more than ideological parables in which good triumphs and social order is always desirable.

The Italian Antonio Gramsci labelled the intersections of ideology and material economic forces 'hegemony', and noted that ideology was to some extent negotiated and consented to by the exploited. Alternatives to the dominant ideology were allowed to circulate through controlled channels, to give the illusion of greater freedom and to let off steam. Education was a means of manufacturing consent and inculcating the ideals of the controlling forces, with the law, courts and prisons as means of enforcing the lesson. It is worth nothing that Gramsci produced much of his work in a prison cell. He saw that cultural texts could potentially manufacture consent or educate the masses into becoming revolutionaries.

In 1916 he defended silent cinema against the charge that it was killing theatre. He felt that theatre had become an industrial practice – indeed, the following year he suggested that if more money could be made by selling peanuts and iced drinks at theatres than putting on plays, they'd likely abandon plays. Silent film was a purer form of theatre, and devoid of the empty intellectual content of the playhouse. Unlike a play, a film would promise little, but delivered equally little.

Gramsci was aware of the ambivalent power of cinema as it developed to reach the masses. There would be audiences which would go to see *Clueless* but would avoid a worthy adaptation of a canonical author.

The Frenchman Louis Althusser discussed Ideological State Apparatuses (ISAs) and Repressive State Apparatuses (RSAs). The ISAs operate as carrots to persuade us to behave in a particular manner – the Church, the family, the legal system, political parties, educational systems, trade unions, media and culture – as if of our own free will, although there is not necessarily much freedom in the choices we make. If the carrots fail, there are the sticks of the RSAs – the government, police forces, law, courts, prisons and the armed forces – to punish us. Film can operate as an ISA.

There are some mentions of the RSAs in *Clueless*, given that Cher's father is a lawyer and part of the legal system; her stepbrother Josh, when trained, will also enter the profession. The school is equally important – although the ISA function of it is rather undercut by a mixture of slacker attitudes and the ability of wealth to buy better grades. The biggest ideological influences upon Cher's life are her father (and his wealth) and Josh. The placing of Cher at its centre as an identificatory figure offers us the chance to identify with someone who is excessively materialist. The rôle of her best friend is played by an African American actress, suggesting that wealth can cut across white, Jewish and African American ethnicities and portraying an equality based on relative wealth. To some extent the greed-is-good ideology is undercut by Josh, and his environmental causes, and the self-revelation that Cher has to come to in order to fall in love with him – however, the political causes reflected in Josh's T-shirts at the start of the film are absent from the end, and he seems to yield to the ideology of his stepfather.

Jean-Luc Comolli and Jean Narboni have argued that every film is political because it is the product of an ideological system. The film may endorse a particular ideological construct such as the idea that the individual matters and can make a difference to the world, the individual can improve him or herself, good will triumph, effort will be rewarded, and financial comfort and a stable marriage are the best reward. It is to be assumed that most Hollywood films endorse these ideologies. Some films do confront ideology by being overtly political, although some of them inadvertently end up supporting dominant ideology after all. Other films confront ideology by subverting or ironising the message, or by appearing to endorse ideology but critiquing it through showing contradictions in the ideas. Some films have a political edge, but end up using conservative forms in which one man is pitting against the system and has a typically bourgeois, middle-class narrative structure. For Comolli and Narboni radical films must have both a political agenda and a radical form. The rôle of the Marxist critic is to expose the ideological blindspots of film, to note the contradictions between form and political content and to engage with any political critique. *Clueless* may be read as ridiculing the love of commodities, but there is no real sense of anyone seriously abandoning all their possessions.

The Frankfurt School

In 1923 a group of Marxist intellectuals set up the Frankfurt Institute for Social Research at Frankfurt University, Germany, with the generosity of businessman Felix Weill. With the rise of Nazism the politics of the school – not to mention the Jewish ethnicity of many of its members – forced it into exile, reconfiguring at Columbia University in 1934 until 1949, when return to a defeated West Germany was possible. Walter Benjamin, sometimes part of the group, was not so lucky and in September 1940 committed suicide on the Franco-Spanish border rather than face being arrested by the Germans. Other members of the school included T.W. Adorno, Erich Fromm, Max Horkheimer, Otto Kirchheimer, Leo Lowenthal, Herbert Marcuse, Franz Neumann and Friedrich Pollock. At the heart of their work was an exploration of the ideological superstructure which includes mass culture.

Adorno in particular wrote of what he called 'the culture industries', which enforced both a standardisation of form – the three-minute pop song, the 90-minute feature film, particular narratives – and a dumbing down of the content. In the name of democratisation the producers of films may be setting out to attract 11-year-olds, but in actuality they are trying to make us into 11-year-olds. Mass culture is like heroin – it appears to solve a need, but it is only a temporary comfort and leaves us wanting more. It makes us feel better and flatters us – and often it appears to include political messages to flatter us as to our intelligence, whereas it is actually keeping any debate under control by acting as an escape valve. A transcendental art was possible – but access to it would involve the revolutionary rearrangement of society.

Clueless, as an uncredited adaptation of Jane Austen's *Emma*, shows the way in which a transcendent work of literature may be repackaged and sold, with a cynical eye on the teenage market. Like the various teen adaptations that were to follow, the film risks making an adult audience into 11-year-olds. On the other hand, it clearly sets out to flatter anyone who recognises the strong parallels between the film and its source. In the end, it does provide feature-length entertainment – but arguably nothing more solid.

Benjamin, in his 'The Work Of Art In The Age Of Mechanical Reproduction', notes how art, in a time of mass production, loses its aura of authenticity and originality – there are now many Mona Lisas, on postcards, posters, T-shirts, mousemats and so forth. And yet film, despite being equally industrial, has a positive function: the spectator of a film is turned into a critic, both of film and reality. The actor is representing him or herself to the mechanical device of the camera, without any feedback from the audience and lacking the aura of a total, theatrical performance. The filmed snippets are sutured together to form a totality observable by an audience, and these inevitably have an impact on the audience – Benjamin is here following Arnheim and Pudovkin. Film, as the first art form which shows that material plays tricks on consumers, can make viewers aware of the problems of representing the material.

Fredric Jameson And Postmodernism

Marxists had argued that the economic base determines the superstructure of a society, so when a new period of capitalism was observed, it followed that a new epoch of culture, ideology, politics and so forth would come into play. Ernest Mandel (1923–1995), for example, divided capitalism into three periods: market, monopoly and postindustrial. The postindustrial period began somewhere between the end of the Second World War in 1945 and the end of reconstruction in the 1960s. The 1960s saw the increasing use of nuclear power and electronic machines, the fall of old empires and the eclipse of the nation-state by multinational corporations. The American academic, Fredric Jameson, was one of several to label the era of the postindustrial as the postmodern age.

For Jameson, the postmodern was to be viewed with a certain amount of suspicion – other theorists would celebrate it. These aesthetics celebrated the copy or simulacrum over the original, style over substance, demonstrated a failure of emotion and individualism, and frequently would be characterised by pastiche or nostalgia for an imagined golden age. Jameson wrote about the nostalgia film in relation to *Star Wars* (1977), *American Graffiti* (1973), *Something Wild* (1986) and *Blue Velvet* (1984). Film, as supposedly a democratic, lowbrow, art form, was written about heavily by postmodern analysts, with *Blade Runner* (1982) being the iconic text for the new iconoclasts.

Whilst you can learn everything you want to learn about this kind of postmodernism (there are others) by watching a Joe Dante movie (or by buying my book on the subject – go on, you know you want to), it can be seen at work in *Clueless*. The rewriting of Austen's *Emma* indicates that there is no possibility of originality anymore, and that Austen's story no longer just belongs to her. We know how it ends because we've read Mills and Boon (Austen for the mass market, and a lot quicker to read, as well as there being many more of them) and we've seen enough romantic comedies to know Emma/Cher'll end up with Mr Knightley/Josh. The joy is in seeing how they get there – in the sexually liberated age there is no reason why Cher could not bed Frank Churchill/Christian, her new male friend, so he is made gay. The valley speak of the characters should not be contrasted with the sophistication of Austen's characters – Cher is actually as sophisticated, or Emma is as vapid. Meanwhile, Austen was being commodified in purer form in *Sense And Sensibility* (1995), *Emma* (1996; with *Trainspotting*'s Renton [Ewan McGregor] as Churchill) and *Mansfield Park* (1999; with *Trainspotting*'s Sick Boy, Jonny Lee Miller). What once was sharp, if hardly revolutionary, social satire, has become Hollywood heritage.

Chapter 5

Semiotics And Structuralism

Ferdinand De Saussure (1857–1915)

The theory of semiotics, also known as semiology or structuralism, in part derives from the lecture notes taken by the students of Ferdinand de Saussure and published as *Course In General Linguistics* (1916). This, naturally, is not a good start. I'd hate for any grand theory to be based on the sort of notes people take in my lectures. Broadly speaking, Saussure's theory involves examining the structure of cultural artefacts by splitting them up into individual bits or signs. Film is, of course, nothing but little bits spliced together.

Saussure returned to a split, observed in Greek philosophy, between the act of representation and a concept being represented. A representation was a sound, letters or a visual image, and was labelled the 'signifier'. The concept being represented by the signifier was the 'signified'. To take an example at random (honest) to explain this, the letters or sound pattern 'd-o-g' represent the idea of a 'dog' – not any actual, real mutt but the *idea* of dog. Saussure would have admitted that there is a real world – he calls it the 'referent' – but argues that our only access to this real world is through language.

Take an example from *Reservoir Dogs* (1991): the signifier Mr White is used to refer to the character played by Harvey Keitel – the signified. Mr White doesn't exist (sorry), but there is an idea of him created by the film. That he is named Mr White is the arbitrary decision of Joe, and no distinction can be predicted between him and Mr Pink. Nor is Mr Pink some mixture of Mr White and an unseen Mr Red. Given that there are only so many colours (short of finding a paint chart and calling someone Mr Moroccan Gold), there may well have been other Mr Whites who have been so designated. Equally, Keitel's character can be called Larry. The signifier–signified relationship may be one to many in both directions. There is therefore a network of signs in relation to each other.

Saussure also argued that signs don't exist in isolation, but are grouped in two dimensions: the syntagmatic and the paradigmatic. The syntagmatic is like syntax, it is the order in which we meet the signs; for example, the order in which we are introduced to Mr White and Mr Orange, Mr Pink, Mr Blonde, Mr Brown and Mr Blue. Certain expectations are set up by syntagmatic structures – which are then adhered to or deviated from by the text. On the scale of the film itself, we don't have the recruitment of the gang, the planning, the heist and then the aftermath, we have the moments before the heist and then the aftermath, before seeing the parallel narratives of Mr White, Mr Pink, Mr Orange and Mr Blonde. The paradigmatic dimension is the choice of one sign over another, i.e. we get Mr White's story but not Mr Brown's or Mr Blue's. There is a whole reservoir of signs to draw on, and the choice of one over another changes the meaning of the text. To leave out Mr Orange's narrative would leave us confused as to why he kills Mr Blonde.

To make the distinction between paradigmatic and syntagmatic more clear, it is worth remembering the different piano styles of northern British comedians Les Dawson and Eric Morecambe. Dawson played the tune but did so by playing the wrong notes. Morecambe famously played the right notes but not necessarily in the right order.

Charles Peirce (1839–1914)

Peirce evolved a parallel system of signifiers and signifieds to Saussure's, based upon sets of three relations between signs and objects, which could be combined to form a bewildering and fiendishly complex system. Fortunately for us, in practice critics only use one of the sets, which deals with the relation of signs to things in the world and is divided into icon, index and symbol.

An icon is where the sign resembles the thing it represents – film itself is iconic because it is a series of photographs of an object. What we see in *Reservoir Dogs* is a series of pictures of Mr Orange, rather than seeing Mr Orange himself. Tim Roth is iconic of Mr Orange, or, rather, pictures of Tim Roth are. (Again it needs to be stated that Mr Orange does not exist.) Perhaps what is important is that the iconic sign needs a member of an audience – a receiver – to recognise the resemblance between sign and object.

The indexical sign is an effect which allows us to infer a cause; the term refers to the habit of pointing things out with the index finger. The blood on Mr Orange's shirt is an index that he has been shot – an event that we do not actually see until towards the end of the film. Equally, many of the events in the film are indexical of a heist, although we never actually see the robbery itself. The indexical sign can be aural rather than visual; as Mr White cradles a dying Mr Orange, we hear police sirens, shouting and a series of shots. It is up to the audience to interpret these sounds, but the chances are that this is Mr Pink's botched escape attempt. We also hear shots and see Mr White's body jerk away but don't see him being shot. Given all this, *Reservoir Dogs* is remarkable for what we don't see – we see the before and after of the slicing of the cop's ear, but not the event itself, bodies riddled with bullets are often obscured by windscreens, and so forth.

Finally, there is the symbolic sign, where the connection between the signifier and the signified is entirely arbitrary – which returns us to the arbitrariness of Mr White being Mr White, rather than any other colour. Or being Larry. There is some habitual linkage between the two but no real sense of causality.

These three kinds of sign don't always remain distinct: icon, index and symbol can be combined in different ways, producing, say, a symbolic icon. Gunfire can just be sport, or it can be defence, or it can be a form of attack. In the case of the gunfire at the end of *Reservoir Dogs* it becomes associated in the viewer's mind with the exit of Mr Pink and therefore is taken to indicate his death, in the same way as we've seen or heard about other characters dying.

This is all very fine, and occasionally splendid, but this seems to just leave us with the film analysed in little bits. It seems necessary to move to some kind of synthesis after this close analysis.

Roland Barthes (1915–1980)

This French structuralist offers us one way into putting the terminology of Saussure and Peirce into action, whilst offering more specialist vocabulary of his own. Barthes' close analysis of both literature and products of popular culture was an attempt to expose the under-lying conservative or bourgeois ideology of what he was studying. In *Mythologies* (1957), he explores adverts for soap powder, kinds of food, movies and other aspects of popular culture.

In 'The Romans In Films' he describes Joseph Mankiewicz's *Julius Caesar* (1953) and the haircuts of the characters; the fringe signifies the Roman nation-ality. Even though the actor is American, this particular hairstyle symbolises a nationality and a place: Caesar's Rome as interpreted by Hollywood via Shakespeare. Further, the characters, except for Julius Caesar, sweat as a sign of their moral state. Caesar is immune to sweating because he is the object of intrigue, rather than a plotter in his own right. Barthes, however, criticises the film for its use of signifiers. He argues that the signifier–signi-fied link should be entirely arbitrary and intellectual, or should be specific to a certain instant and location, spontaneously revealing the signified. The haircut and sweat, for Barthes, show too clearly the hand of the hairdressing and make-up departments rather than reality or pure artifice. Because the film falls between these twin poles, it is a degraded spectacle.

Barthes develops his examination of bourgeois ideology at length, arguing that culture attempts to portray itself as natural, traditional, authentic and fixed, rather than as arbitrary – just what happens to be the case. In the process he reverses the idea that the sign is divided into a signifier and a signified, and argues that the sign is the *product* of signifier and signified. He notes that the process of signification is not a two-term system – where gunshots signify someone being shot – but a three-term one: the *signifier*, the *signified* and the *sign* which is the connecting of the two. Gunshots, after all, can just be a gun being shot, but these particular gunshots become a sign when Mr Pink is killed.

This sign is part of the process of language; it operates within the realm of 'denotation'. The signifier and signified 'denote' something. But this sign is simply the first sign. The sign which is the killing of Mr Pink becomes in turn a further signifier. This new signifier, associated with a further signified, produces a second sign, which is part of a metalanguage, or what Barthes called 'mythology'. This second sign operates on the level of 'connotation'. The killing of Mr Pink might be said to be a signifier for the signified of criminals being punished – and the second sign 'connotes' that criminals are punished for their misdeeds, that crime does not pay, that order will assert itself.

For all its formal experimentation, for all its placing of criminals at the centre of the narrative, *Reservoir Dogs* does not allow its anti-heroes to escape with the diamonds. Instead, Mr Blue, Mr Brown, Mr Blonde, Nice Guy Eddie, Joe, Mr White and Mr Pink are shot and killed. There is no honour among thieves and criminals will not prosper. The only character who might possibly survive – depending on whether his bleeding can be stopped, is Mr Orange, the undercover cop. And this seems unlikely because he has killed an innocent civilian.

V I Propp (1895–1970)

V I Propp's structuralist study of Russian fairy tales discovered that they all had the same basic narrative – that there is a basic order of signs or syntagm which we recognise. We need to make a distinction between story and plot. The story is the sequence of events which occur to a number of characters in chronological order. The plot is the order in which these are unveiled to the audience, with some events being left to be inferred rather than being portrayed on screen. Often at the start of a story there is a sense of status quo, which is then threatened – something is prohibited by law, perhaps, and someone breaks the rules. After a period of chaos, if the status quo cannot be restored, then at least a new equilibrium is reached.

Star Wars (1977) seems a good place to start. Whilst Luke is out in the desert, his adoptive family is killed and so he wants revenge. At the end of the movie he has acquired a new family – Han, Chewbacca, the droids and Leia. The story of *Reservoir Dogs* is obscured by its plot, but it could be summarised as the disruption of law and order by a diamond heist restored by the killing of all the thieves.

V I Propp argued that each narrative consists of 31 functions – a function here being an action by a character which has significance for the story. These functions are distributed around seven different spheres, each corresponding to a character type: the villain, the donor, the helper, the sought-for person/princess and her father, the dispatcher, the hero and the false hero. Individual 'people' can actually fulfil different kinds of function at different points in the narrative, and therefore can be different characters; equally several 'people' can fulfil the same function. The seven spheres are a narrative sign system.

An imaginary narrative might be constructed to illustrate the seven spheres. A father sends someone to rescue his daughter from the clutches of a villain but this fails. The true hero, who has been secretly in love with the daughter, is sent out next, with his faithful companion. Along the way he meets a wise old man, who gives him a magical object. The hero defeats the villain with the use of the object and makes his escape with the princess in a hot air balloon through the mouth of a volcano as the villain's undersea base is destroyed.

Such a structure is difficult to equate with *Reservoir Dogs*, particularly given the lack of any substantial female character who could be anything approaching a princess. If Mr Orange is the hero, then Eddie and Joe are the sought-for person and father, their fellow cops are the helpers, dispatchers and donors, Mr Blonde is the villain and Mr White is, perhaps, the false hero. The others – Messrs Pink, Blue and Brown – are window dressing.

Star Wars offers a clearer example, with Luke as the hero, searching for Princess Leia. In his quest he is helped by C3PO and R2D2 (the latter also acting as dispatcher) and is donated a light sabre by Obi Wan. Han Solo is the false hero and Darth Vader the villain. Leia acts as her own dispatcher, via R2D2, and Darth Vader turns out to be her father (and indeed Luke's).

Naturally this results in severe simplifications of narratives – which is of course the point. And not all films fit the narrative. The romantic comedy begins with two people antagonistic to each other and ends with the two of them married – whether it be an adaptation of Jane Austen or a screwball comedy such as *Bringing Up Baby* (1938). We could say that the film reinforces the structure by the amount that it deviates from it – but that fails to be satisfactory as well. The other problem is that this kind of analysis pins too much on a narrative being about one person, rather than being a series of interlocking narratives about different people; it would be impossible to reduce *Crash* (2004) to a simplistic, single, linear story, no matter how much the plot was restructured into chronological order.

Antinomies

In Chapter 3 I noted that Peter Wollen was responsible for structuralist *auteurism*, and so it might be worth repeating and expanding this position briefly here. A film can consist of any number of events selected from the infinite number of events that could be depicted – this is operating on a paradigmatic level. A particular kind of selection – Westerns, musicals, certain sorts of shot, for example – might be designated as the work of a given director. Alternatively, a certain sort of structure (syntagm) – the thriller, the romantic comedy – might be thought of as typical of a certain director.

Wollen argued that particular films were ideological battlegrounds for antinomies. An antinomy is one of a pair of binary opposites; it is a signified, but one which is defined in relation to a signified that is its opposite. The temptation of a structuralist reading is to pin down a film or other text into a single, stable meaning, privileging one set of poles – civilised, moral, detective and so on – over the other. Any reading has to be alert to the complexity of the oppositions, and how characters manoeuvre between them.

This kind of reading is one which has been unhelp-fully labelled 'post-structuralist', but is in fact even more structuralist: the much misunderstood idea of decon-struction, as described by Jacques Derrida. Deconstruction isn't just a case of taking a film to pieces, it is taking it to pieces in a particular way. Nor does it declare the author (or I guess, here, the director) to be dead. The deconstructive reading is one which takes the intention of a particular author and shows how the details of the text both support and, more crucially, undermine it.

To return to the point that a signifier can point to several signifieds, a number of characters point out that their names have got unsavoury connotations – in particular Mr Pink's sense that he is being labelled homosexual. The film silences this set of connotations, insisting on the arbitrariness of the naming. A decon-structive reading would be one which brings out these connotations, which might see the film as a love story between men – with Mr Pink acting as some kind of distraction. To turn to Fincher, it is not that *Seven* (1995) inverts society's hierarchy which privileges civilised over savage, so that the film privileges savage over civilised, but thanks to the film it becomes impos-sible to define the terms 'savage' and 'civilised' in the same way as before.

Christian Metz

Metz is a theorist whose ideas link together structuralism and psychoanalysis in terms of the way that cinema works. I will briefly refer to him in the section on Lacan and the Mirror Phase in the next chapter. His debt to structuralism comes from his assertion that cinema is different from other kinds of texts because it is not purely aural or visual, and so it is more complex to isolate the individual sign. At first, he tried to break films into discrete chunks that could be analysed, and which fitted together in a linear or syntagmatic order. The hierarchy of different chunks gave way to a hierarchy of codes, some of which were purely cinematic, some of which were common to other media.

The next phase of Metz's concepts drew on Lacan's ideas. The image of an object or a character in a film doesn't signify that this is an object or a character, but rather announces that *here* is that object or that character. The process of presentation is visible rather than hidden, with a beam of light between projector and screen. It's a signifier but one which serves to distance the viewer from reality. This distance produces or unveils a lack within the viewer, a viewer who is transformed into a voyeur. To understand this idea, it is better to turn more directly to the ideas of Freud and Lacan.

Chapter 6

Psychoanalysis

Psychoanalysis is an approach to the cinema which really came to the fore in the 1970s, in particular with Laura Mulvey's article 'Visual Pleasure And Narrative Cinema' (1975), one of the most significant pieces of film theory. Psychoanalytic film theory builds upon the ideas of Sigmund Freud (1856–1939) and his followers, such as Carl Jung (1875–1961), Ernest Jones (1879–1958), Melanie Klein (1882–1960), Joan Rivière (1883–1962) and, most importantly, Jacques Lacan (1901–1981). It can be used to analyse film characters as if they are real people or case studies, to analyse the director's personality (putting too much weight upon the director's contribution at the expense of the other crewmembers) and to examine the mechanisms of cinema itself. This is clearly too much material to deal with here, so I will focus on Freud, Lacan and Mulvey, returning to some of these ideas in the chapter on feminism.

The theory is not without its critics, most notably from those on the political left who argue that it is the impact of society on the individual which matters in determining behaviour, rather than inner psychic conflicts. Freud's analysis of human sexuality could be considered sexist and homophobic, although that has not stopped some feminist critics from using his ideas. Further, it often seems to be contradicted by the last century of scientific examination of the brain and personal experience – and the influence of middle-class patriarchal Vienna upon Freud's thinking should not be underestimated. After all, how accurate can a theory of human behaviour be if it is based upon the actions of those who are identified as mentally ill or sick? Nevertheless, psychoanalytic structures do seem to describe a surprising number of films.

The Return Of The Repressed

For Freud, all human behaviour derived from the need for gratification – this is the Pleasure Principle, with desires arising from the unconscious mind. The unconscious is part of the mind that determines what we do and feel, although we cannot access it directly – otherwise it wouldn't be unconscious. If we performed every unconscious desire then anarchy would result: no work would get done, no food would be produced, rape would be endemic and, well, we'd all be exhausted. Society therefore frowns upon such sexual excess and so the individual represses desires – this is the Reality Principle.

Simply because a desire is repressed, however, doesn't mean that it goes away. Think of the desire as a flow of water, and the repression as a dam built across it. The water doesn't stop flowing: pressure builds up, and so the water will find a way round, over or eventually through the blockage. Therefore there needs to be some kind of sluice to regulate the pressure. Repressed desires will emerge in the forms of dreams, jokes, slips of the tongue (parapraxes), hallucinations and even physical symptoms. This becomes evident in *Fight Club* (1999). In some moments when the narrator loses control of his body, he beats himself up.

The return of the repressed is central to the under-standing of much horror film, in particular variants on the slasher movie such as *Halloween* (1978), *A Nightmare On Elm Street* (1984) and *I Know What You Did Last Summer* (1997). In these films a crime has happened in the past, and has been forgotten about by the commu-nity; many years later someone comes back to seek revenge, usually on nubile young teenagers. Anyone who has had extramarital sex is marked out for death – at the end of the movie a plucky female virgin faces down the villain alone. A society's fear – about sexuality in general, about female and child sexuality, about race and about class – is projected onto a villainous other, who proceeds to attempt to destroy that society. There is more about the slasher film in the chapter on genre.

The Oedipus Complex

Freud argued that the child goes through different sexualities before settling down as an adult. Initially there is the oral phase, where pleasure derives from suckling at the breast; arguably the distinction between child and parent is barely maintained at this point. Next, the anal phase enables the child to explore its bodily boundaries; the control of the flow of faeces and urine causes degrees of pleasure and displeasure, in particular with the delayed discharge of faeces. Then the child discovers that pleasure can be obtained from playing with their sexual organs. Parents, on the whole, try to put a stop to such behaviour. After this point there is a latent period before so-called proper genital sexuality can commence.

In the meantime, the child is desirous of the mother, as the primary source of pleasure, but is threatened with castration either directly by the father, threatened by the mother on his behalf ('wait until your father gets home'), or just feels threatened. The male child has to disengage from the relationship with the mother and, having squared off with the father, can only hope to find power and happiness by finding a woman to replace his mother. This process is all part of the Oedipus complex, which Freud draws from the Greek myth of the man who married his mother and killed his father.

The trajectory of the female is much more controversial; Freud quickly rubbished the Electra complex – which attempted to reverse the sexes – but never quite settled on his own explanation. The female child is still in this Oedipal relationship with the mother and is threatened with castration. Ah, but as the female lacks a penis she is either castrated or – having a clitoris – comparatively underendowed. The female then will attempt to seduce the father, to gain access to his penis (or, rather, because we're as much talking about notions of power as of anatomy, his phallus). The incest taboo prevents the father–daughter relationship from developing sexually, and so she turns to other men, in the hope of gaining a phallus through having a child of her own. (I have to note that I've always found that men are anxious about castration, whereas women deny their penis envy. Clearly they are repressing it.)

The successful negotiation of the Oedipus complex

results in a heterosexual identity – its failure might result in bisexuality, homosexuality or other medical conditions. Neither the narrator nor Tyler Durden in *Fight Club* seem particularly well adjusted, and both of them have had problematic relationships with their fathers. They have both been raised by their mothers, and therefore may not have successfully negotiated the complex. Both have trouble with authority figures, resulting in violent actions on their parts.

Id, Ego And Superego

In the 1920s Freud began to write of a three-part structure to the mind, although it had at least five parts. There was the conscious Perception System, the Preconscious, consisting of things forgotten, the Ego (part preconscious, part unconscious), the entirely unconscious Id, and 'between' the last two, the Superego.

The Id is formed from the desires of the individual and can be seen in the untrammelled behaviour of Tyler Durden – who steals, screws and hurts what he wants. When he has a desire he acts upon it, even if this causes pain or inconvenience to others. This should be contrasted with the Ego as represented by the narrator, who noticeably fails to take advantage of Marla when he is examining her breasts for cancer, who has to be cajoled into hitting Tyler and who has a reasonably comfortable lifestyle courtesy of the IKEA catalogue. Between the two of them, presumably, is the real Tyler Durden, who has been traumatised by some event into having a split personality – one half entirely Ego, the other Id.

This leaves the Superego to account for, which is formed out of the wreckage of the Oedipus complex and is created by introjecting patriarchal power into the psyche. The Superego is the regulator of pleasure — it will censor the Id, but it will also license it. In *Fight Club* the Superego occurs in a number of forms; initially the self-help groups (which allow him some sleep), then the fight clubs (which allow acts of aggression) and Project Mayhem. The Superego may also be identified with the police, who enter the narrative at various moments of crisis.

Fetishism, Voyeurism And Scopophilia

And thus to another controversial point: castration and the fetish. At some point the male child realises that his mother, and women in general, are castrated. Okay, clearly on anything other than a symbolic level women aren't, but I'm not saying the child is correct. The woman's castration is a constant reminder to the male child of the possibility of his castration, which is, to say the least, disturbing. In some situations, the male will latch onto some item to act as a substitute phallus, which simultaneously will disavow the possibility of castration, and act as a reminder that it might happen.

The object might be a part of somebody else's body (breast, legs, even a shiny nose), a piece of clothing (often shoes, underwear, occasionally gloves) or even objects. If *Fight Club*'s narrator is a fetishist, then it's for his material lifestyle, his yin and yang table and so forth. He overcomes his fetish by destroying these objects only to plunge into a deeper split of personality.

As women in Freud's theories are already castrated,

they cannot become fetishists – something that feminist critics of the 1990s disputed. If this structure is to be followed, then cinema, built up from shots which fetishise the human body, is gendered masculine. This is something I will return to later in my discussion of Laura Mulvey.

The act of looking can itself be perverse – as voyeurism or scopophilia. If all that is looked at is the genitals (and note the flashframes of genitals that Tyler smuggles into films), if looking is part of overcoming nausea or if it replaces intercourse as a source of pleasure, then this looking should be considered as perverse. Voyeurism is thus a kind of sexuality derived from looking at things or people, but scopophilia takes it a stage further and takes in sadism. Scopophilia treats the people being looked at as objects, ideally under our control, and it is even better for the person looking at them if they are suffering. In *Fight Club* there is at least one moment when the narrator shifts into scopophilia, for example when he attacks the blond boy in the basement and takes pleasure in seeing him hurt. His connection to the act stops it from being scopophilia, but if we've begun to identify with him then we are voyeurs.

Cinema, after all, is obsessed with cinema and many hundreds of films draw attention to the act of looking. *Fight Club*, with its moment of the narrator talking directly to the camera and pointing out the cigarette burns which mark a reel changeover, is no exception. The classic study of scopophilia (or scoptophilia as the film calls it) is Michael Powell's *Peeping Tom* (1960), complete with a scopophile who gets his kicks from watching the footage of himself murdering women.

Because it is a substitute for the sexual act, it can never be enough to satisfy him and he is driven to repeat his crimes.

Jacques Lacan

Lacan was a French psychoanalyst who felt that Freud had been misinterpreted by his followers. In his return to Freud he was to be influenced by the ideas of structuralism, partly the anthropology of Levi-Strauss and the signifier/signified split. It is traditional to point out that Lacan is difficult and that some of the translations of his work are poor, but in the transcriptions of his seminars he also emerges as a very witty person.

Lacan solves one criticism that can be aimed at Freud's versions of the Oedipus complex: what about single-parent or same-sex families who seem to be able to produce well-adjusted individuals? The father is here replaced by the phallus – also a signifier for our patriarchal society – and the Name of the Father, which functions with the threat of castration. Anyone – an uncle, a stepfather, a woman, even the mother – can function as the phallus.

The child desires to be desired by the mother but the mother desires the phallus. The child therefore attempts to become a phallus for the mother and to become the centre of her world. The child fails and the result differs according to sex. The male is reassured that even if he's failed now, one day all this will be his, he may yet become the phallus. In the meantime, he has the compensation of language, which Lacan calls the symbolic order. The female cannot fully access the symbolic order (which is patriarchal) and can only console herself with thoughts of a time before she was castrated ... But this, perhaps, is to get ahead of ourselves.

The Mirror Phase And The Imaginary

For Lacan, we are born too soon. We can't walk, talk or see. We begin as broken people. At some point, however, we encounter an image of ourselves in a mirror and begin to identify ourselves as a distinct person in the world, separate from others. The image seems to be better than us and is external to ourselves, so this identification is problematic in itself. This process is the Mirror Phase and it allows us to enter into the realm of the Imaginary – with the emphasis being on the idea of the image.

This Mirror Phase can act as a metaphor for what we do in the cinema – and this idea was developed by Christian Metz. We sit in the dark, quietly (Metz clearly doesn't go to your average multiplex), and don't move, whilst watching an image of a person who is much bigger, stronger, more intelligent, braver and more resourceful than ourselves. The mirror of the cinema screen doesn't reflect us back but shows whom we'd like to be. I'm no Brad Pitt, but I wouldn't mind being him (well, aside from in *Meet Joe Black* (1998)).

The Symbolic Order And The Real

As part of the Mirror Phase the individual becomes anchored in language – he or she is spoken to or spoken of, and is located in time, space and language. This language is to be understood in terms of Saussure's network of signifiers and signifieds, as explored in Chapter 5. Signifiers can be exchanged for other signifiers in an endless chain of signification. (To understand this try looking a word up in the dictionary – any word will do. The definition will offer you more words, which need to be defined, and so on. Either you will get stuck in a loop of definitions, or end up chasing meanings through the whole dictionary.)

After the child has gone through the Mirror Phase, the Oedipus complex follows and the child faces the signifier of the phallus or Name Of The Father. The male child emerges from this and can enter the Symbolic Order – one day he will be associated with the phallus, but in the meantime he must make do with the system of exchange that includes the patriarchal social system. In contrast, the female child can only console herself with the (fake) memory of the time before she was castrated, when she was associated with the phallus, and cannot fully enter into the Symbolic Order.

From a feminist point of view, this is as problematic as Freud's analysis, but some feminists such as Julia Kristeva have argued that women must find their own, non-patriarchal order or language of babble, which she calls the semiotic. Most films follow a masculine structure, a linear narrative which begins with a disruption to the social order, and then various attempts to reinstate it successfully. A feminine structure might be different – see for example the works of Sally Potter and Jane Campion, or even Derek Jarman, where episode outweighs the entire story.

Aside from the Imaginary and the Symbolic, Lacan posits the dimension of the Real, which is that which exists before and beyond language, and cannot be symbolised. The Real might occur during sex, or after death, or before birth. The Real is the moment when Tyler Durden is a unified whole, before his breakdown, or the flashframes which intervene in the first half of the film, or the moment when you appear to see the edges of the film.

Laura Mulvey And The Gaze

Lacan's ideas are important to film studies in part because they inform much feminist thought, but also because Mulvey's 'Visual Pleasure And Narrative Cinema' draws upon them. Mulvey takes the idea of the member of the audience watching a film, and argues that what begins as an identificatory gaze slides into something more sadistic. Yes, we identify with Brad Pitt in the fight club but we also want to see him being beaten up by the gangster boss. In order for there to be a narrative – and most of us want a narrative in our movies – people must suffer, including the hero. Durden must suffer, the narrator must suffer.

At the same time there is a sense of discomfort at looking at the woman on screen – in this case Marla, as played by Helena Bonham Carter. Woman is castrated and so looking at woman reminds the viewer of the possibility of being castrated. Marla's attendance at a testicular cancer support group, her constant smoking, put her as being beyond the control of Norton's character, and his life is disrupted by her until he finds something to substitute for the therapy groups. Somehow the hero's dealings with the castrated female are meant to allay the viewer's fears.

Mulvey argues that there are three kinds of look associated with the cinema: a diegetic one between the characters, an extradiegetic one of the audience watching the film, and then the look of the crew filming the events played out before the camera. In Hollywood cinema all three kinds of gaze are predominantly masculine, or associated with the male, and part of what Mulvey was arguing for was an alternative form of cinema. She does rather make the assumption that everyone, male or female, straight or gay, will go along with the identification, and that these structures are at work throughout Hollywood cinema. Since then she has written an afterword which qualifies this gendering of cinema but in my opinion she doesn't get much beyond the idea of a male gaze. A female gaze should, of course, be possible, but it is best to postpone discussion of this to the next chapter.

Chapter 7

Feminism

Feminism is an area of thought, philosophy and politics that covers a variety of areas within film studies: canon formation, representations of women, representations of gender (more properly sexual) inequalities between women and men, the gendered construction of the viewer and the possibilities for female cinema. Before looking at these areas in turn, some terminology would be useful.

Female, Feminine, Feminist

Being female is something which is biologically determined – in particular by the twenty-third pair of chromosomes that fix the child's sex. This results in anatomical features developing differently between the sexes: breasts, ovaries, the vagina and so forth. Almost all people are born either female or male and stay that way all their lives; an increasing fraction of the population has both female and male organs. Surgery can convert a person's anatomical sex, but this would not impact upon the genetics. Theorists who insist on the fixed differences between women and men are known as essentialists.

The feminine is a social construction just as the masculine is. Feminine qualities are traditionally considered to be passivity, modesty, nurturing and feeling, whereas masculine qualities are activity, exhibitionism, uncaring and thinking. These are characteristics that our society (specifically late twentieth and early twenty-first century Western society) assumes that females and males will have. Females can have masculine qualities and males have feminine qualities but society has often frowned upon this, taking it as a sign of some kind of perversion or homosexuality, of being not quite proper.

Feminism is the name given to a whole raft of thought and political movements that have been primarily concerned with the position of women and men in society. Feminism is opposed to sexism – which can be used to describe the whole series of ways in which women are degraded and undermined, primarily by men. (Some women can also be anti-women or tacitly consent to their own oppression.) Not all women are feminists and not all feminists are women.

There are those who say that the pendulum has swung too far and that men are actually oppressed within society. This may be true, in that men were the primary breadwinners during the twentieth century and so have been at the forefront of work-related alienation, and have suffered through class inequality. Further, there has been a worrying decline in male educational achievement. Policies of quotas or positive discrimination necessarily mean that men are seen as losing out. Nevertheless, women remain outnumbered at senior levels – in the boardroom, law court, parliament and so forth. Women still earn less than men in movies and it is still difficult to name more than a handful of female film directors.

The Canon

At the risk of sounding like a wimp, my selection of films has been somewhat pitiful from a feminist point of view: *Seven* (1995), *Fight Club* (1999), *The Usual Suspects* (1995) and *Reservoir Dogs* (1991). In *Seven* the only significant speaking rôle for a woman is Gwyneth Paltrow's Tracey – a passive, caring victim appearing in a handful of scenes, with no life outside her home (aside from a visit to a diner). In *Fight Club* Marla is a character with some dubious morals who borders on the psychopathic. Keaton's wife in *The Usual Suspects* is hardly a substantial part. And the only woman that I can recall in *Reservoir Dogs* is torn screaming from her car. Not a good start, really. There was *Clueless*, but perhaps that is tokenism.

The majority of directors and producers in Hollywood are male. This probably holds true in cinemas around the world. The movies that get the publicity budgets are made within male genres – block-busters, war, science fiction or thrillers. These films seem to figure a central male character who is facing a male villain, and has a male best friend (who often gets killed by the villain in the penultimate reel, justifying the hero's killing of the villain). The female characters are there to titillate, to be in distress and be rescued, and occasionally to guarantee the heterosexuality of the hero. (See chapter 8.)

This male dominance is true of almost all cultural productions – all have far more male creators than female. There's some ideology at work in society that suggests that female narratives are too particular, domestic, or narrow to have wide appeal, whereas male narratives are universal, outgoing and broad. Even if a woman does manage to make a film, it is still difficult to break through and make a second or third. The canon of films embraced by audiences and critics remains predominantly male. The director discussed in this chapter, Patricia Rozema, has made it to four; an interest in passive or quiet women who start to fight for what they want appears to be emerging.

One explanation – not a justification – is that men go to the cinema to identify with the male hero and to ogle the female characters. The women in the audience, brought in tow by the men, are used to having to imagine themselves as male. This is a caricature of the version of cinema put forward and critiqued by Laura Mulvey in 'Visual Pleasures And Narrative Cinema'. The end of narrative cinema – which Mulvey would probably like to see – would be a feminist move.

Representation Of Women In Film

In the past there were few rôles that women played in films: angelic mothers, castrating mothers, crones, victims, girlfriends, whores and *femmes fatales*. In several of these stereotypes the character is not an agent in the narrative, but a counter in the ongoing male-centred narrative. In the latter two cases there is more involvement in affecting the storyline, but these are hardly positive rôles. The question is whether the filmmakers are endorsing these portrayals or merely reflecting a society in which few rôles can be envisaged for females.

The angelic mother is a continuation of the nineteenth-century conception of the angel of the house, who stays at home, rears children and is the solid rock of the hearth. Whilst the male goes out and faces great adventures and trials, her lifestyle is being fought for. Fanny Price's mother in Rozema's *Mansfield Park* (1999) seems to have little life beyond children and sending her eldest child off to have a better life. She offers Fanny an awful warning of what might happen if you marry for love. However, she is a more positive portrayal of motherhood than Mrs Bertram, who is continuously drunk or high on opium (presumably laudanum), often dozes and only dotes on her pet dog. Certainly there is no sense that she has imbued her children with morals. She is never sinister enough to be a castrating mother figure – one who undercuts the authority and power of her husband or children. The crone may sometimes be a figure of great wisdom (the grandmother in *Company Of Wolves* (1984)) or a garrulous gossip, prone to snap moral judgments and in the end a figure of ridicule (Mrs Norris in *Mansfield Park*).

It is telling that Fanny Price is not as much a victim in the film as in the original novel – although in both cases they get to marry Edmund Bertram. In the book she is much more placid and passive, and left to her fate, although in both cases she is guided by a moral conviction that will make things come right in the end. The film builds up her spirit, and her willingness to answer back – I'm almost tempted to use the word feisty. What remains clear is that she is always someone else's property – her mother's to give away, Sir Thomas Bertram's or Mrs Norris's to order around, or Henry Crawford's to marry. Her rejection of Henry's proposal leads to her temporary eviction from the quasi-paradise of Mansfield Park. The ending, in which there is the suggestion that she will become a writer, is certainly a late twentieth-century imposition on her union.

Even in a version of Austen that has a feminist spin, there is the sense that the narrative punishes the most whore-like character. Sir Thomas's daughter Maria is already engaged to the foolish Rushworth – a man of means – when she encounters Henry, who by rights should be an eligible suitor for her sister Julia. Rather than consummate this new passion, she marries hurriedly, but cannot contain herself forever. The scandal seems more likely to ruin her than Henry, who does go on to marry. She is sent into exile with Mrs Norris, and this is deemed to be punishment for them both.

The *femme fatale* overlaps with the whore. Both are powerful, self-assured women who can turn the hero's life upside down. Often cold and apparently emotionless, the *femme fatale* is the object of sexual attraction for the male. These figures most often occurred in *films noirs* of the 1940s and 1950s, and made a return in 1990s *neo noirs*. John Dahl created notable examples in *Red Rock West* (1992) and *The Last Seduction* (1993), in which unwary males put their trust in an attractive woman, only to risk taking the fall for a crime that she has committed. In the latter, Linda Fiorentino's character is even able to get away with it. More recently, in films like *A Life Less Ordinary* (1997), *Very Bad Things* (1998) and to some extent *Being John Malkovich* (1999), Cameron Diaz has turned psychopath on unwary males or has proved to be more immoral than they are. Mary Crawford, in *Mansfield Park*, is a more decorous version, scheming to get one of the Bertram sons or, rather, their fortune, almost on the edge of seducing Fanny, and unscrupulous in her actions. She ends up in what looks like a marriage of convenience.

Representation Of Inequalities

Films seem to represent the wider notion of culture that women only really have an existence in relation to men – at worst they are the property of their fathers until they marry, when they become property of their husbands. Women's interests are often deemed too peripheral, too provincial or too domestic to be of interest in a film. Meanwhile, a large number of narratives have women as backdrop to the main business. Even narratives with women at their centres, suffering the arrows of outrageous fortune, the misfortune is often caused by a man, and all too often a man solves the problem rather than allowing the woman to be the agent of her own redemption. Time and again women are represented as unequal to men, especially physically – and a strong woman is shown as a monster.

Spielberg's version of *The Color Purple* (1985) is a sanitised version of a moving novel about the physical and sexual abuse suffered by a young black female at the hands of men; her salvation for once lies in finding the company of women. There's an uncomfortable moment in *Blade Runner* (1982) when Rick Deckard all but rapes Rachael, a replicant. She is, after all, a variation on Pris, a basic sex model and that would appear to be her function, but the other female replicants show greater strength. Deckard slams the door so that she can't leave his apartment and demands that she asks that he kiss her, and then demands that she says that she loves him. Scott fortunately cuts away from this forced seduction.

Women also find themselves unequal outside the home, particularly in the workplace. In *Working Girl*

(1988) Melanie Griffith faces the indignity of being given the chance to sleep her way to the top (with Kevin Spacey, no less), and then hopes she can further her career by working with Sigourney Weaver. Weaver portrays a successful woman who has pulled the ladder up after her; far from helping Griffith she tries to take credit for the initiative shown by her assistant. Plucky Griffith comes through in the end, although it's rather tempting to think that she's slept her way to the top (with Harrison Ford's character).

The Gendered Construction Of The Viewer

Even when Mulvey revisited her article on 'Visual Pleasure And Narrative Cinema' she barely constructed a female viewer. The female viewer, trained by the male gaze of the director and the characters on the screen, has to cross-dress at the movies and become a man for the occasion.

The reverse also seems to be the case in the one genre to have consistently presented strong female leads in the last 30 years: the slasher horror film. From *Halloween* (and its near contemporary, *Alien* (1979)) to the *Scream* trilogy and *The Blair Witch Project* (1998), a female has been put at the centre of the narrative and is either the last to survive or one of the few to survive. Laurie is left to face Michael Myers alone, Ripley goes face to face with Aliens and then the Alien Queen. In *Scream* the film jerks note what has long been acknowledged in horror criticism: the virgin is saved, the sexual woman is killed. Laurie's refusal of a date guarantees her survival, whereas her fellow babysitter who has been fooling around is dead meat. Whilst the point-of-view shots might encourage some identification with the (usually) male villain, the central character for audience empathy is female. Given that the audience for this type of film is predominantly male, is it that the male is cross-dressing, as it were, and becoming feminine for the evening? Or is it some more sinister voyeurism that is attracted by seeing young women in peril? (I will return to this topic in the chapter on genre.)

Possibilities For A Female Cinema

There have been female directors in the past – such as Dorothy Arzner or Ida Lupino – but most of these are neglected. But even if the director is female, it doesn't necessarily follow that the director is a feminist. In *Blue Steel* (1989), *Point Break* (1991) and *Strange Days* (1995) Kathryn Bigelow proves that she can have as much testosterone as any male director. Even when in the first film she puts a woman at the centre – Jamie Lee Curtis – it is hardly a traditional female figure.

There are also moments in the output of male directors that can offer women visual pleasure. In Howard Hawks's comedies it is a truism that the females control the men – Cary Grant's life is turned upside down by Katharine Hepburn in *Bringing Up Baby* (1938). In *Gentlemen Prefer Blondes* (1953) material needs outweigh the need for a man – diamonds are a girl's best friend. Marilyn Monroe in the film appears to be a dumb blonde but admits to her fiancé's father that her dumb little girl act is there to reassure men and enable her to get her own way. The closing image is of two women getting married – admittedly not to each other, but both seem firmly in charge.

The psychoanalyst Joan Rivière has argued that womanliness is a masquerade, a performance, which maintains a balance between male and female. To reassure the male ego, the woman pretends to be more attractive (that is, stupid) than she really is. Some 60 years after Rivière, the writings of Judith Butler argue that all gender is something which is performed, and recent cinema seems to endorse this. In *The Adventures Of Priscilla, Queen Of The Desert* (1994) Terence Stamp performs a transsexual who performs a drag act. His fellow artiste, played by Hugo Weaving, performs masculinity in a cowboy suit. In films directed by Almodóvar there are women cast as men who have had surgery to become women, and men who have had surgery to become women cast as men, and men pretending to be men. In Kimberley Peirce's *Boys Don't Cry* (1999), a woman performs a woman trying to pass as a boy.

Certain genres are of particular interest to women – what *Sleepless In Seattle* (1993) cruelly labels chick flicks. Melodrama and romantic comedy have been traditional favourites, the former tending to focus on the threat to the family posed by masculine law or a particular male, the latter on the tribulations of a woman falling in love with a man she hates and who often hates her. Given that the latter usually ends with a marriage, these are certainly not straightforwardly feminist, if at all.

The strongest contribution to feminist cinema has come from the independent sector, where low or zero budgets have led to experimental films which are, sadly, unlikely to find a wider audience. Jane Campion had made several movies in Australia or New Zealand before she made the art cinema success, *The Piano* (1993), a film with a silent woman at the centre, a metaphor for her lack of power and agency. Rose Troche and Guinevere Turner had an indie hit with their low-budget lesbian film, *Go Fish* (1994), again a film which is unlikely to have mainstream success but which repays a look.

In part because of their conditions of production – shooting in brief periods when equipment or money is available – many of these films are episodic. This form is probably suitable for feminist materials. Thinkers such as Hélène Cixous, Julia Kristeva and Lucie Irigaray, drawing on Lacan, have proposed the possibility of a feminine style. The male child passes into the Symbolic Order as a result of the Oedipus complex, having a male-centred language at his disposal. The female cannot use this language comfortably and is left with babble. This babble is episodic, allusive, discontinuous, cosmic, fluid and reaches multiple climaxes.

One example of this is Sally Potter's *Orlando* (1992), based on Virginia Woolf's novel. Tilda Swinton plays the male Orlando, who lives for over 400 years, and at one point in history wakes up as a woman and is dispossessed of home and title. The film is a series of episodes, each focusing on a different aspect of life and relationships between the sexes, and with Orlando as the only character to be in every chapter. The film, beautifully shot, and well performed, is nevertheless easy to resist: we are just not used to seeing such structures. Having been exposed for so long to masculine film language, the feminine is difficult to take. Potter's *The Man Who Cried* (2000), starring Christina Ricci, Johnny Depp and Cate Blanchett, welds a Hollywood ending onto arthouse tragedy, an ending which feels so consolatory that it almost needs to be viewed as a fantasy.

Chapter 8

Queer Theory

Part of the project of feminist film criticism is to identify the different kinds of screen representation of women. Whilst there are some moments of ambiguity, it is usually possible to identify a woman. It is less easy to unambiguously locate homosexual characters. Some might be regarded as such by the viewer even though they never engage in any homosexual act. Indeed, some characters can be identified as homosexual even though they engage in heterosexual acts. Something queer is going on.

The word 'Queer' has come to signify a whole range of sexualities other than heterosexual: gay, lesbian, bisexual, transsexual and so forth. It is a word which until the 1980s had mainly derogatory connotations, but in political and protest movements it has come to be a token of collective identity, resistance and even pride. We're here, we're queer, you've got a problem with that? A queer reading of a film is one that exposes the hidden desires between members of the same sex. In this chapter I will examine the concept of the homosexual, the parallel ideas of homosociality and fratriarchy, the history of differing depictions of gays on film and the structure of the buddy movie, as well as notions of camp.

The Homosexual

In *Bringing Up Baby* (1938) Cary Grant's character has been forced to wear a female dressing gown and feather boa when the doorbell rings. The woman in tweeds who has arrived seems nonplussed, as Grant explains 'I've just gone gay all of a sudden.' Forty years earlier, a short film featuring two men was called *The Gay Brothers* (1895). Does the word 'gay' in these two cases mean homosexual – or bright, cheerful and light-hearted? Is there a double entendre in Grant's line? 'Gay' is usually thought of as deriving from the 1960s, possibly from the acronym for 'Good As You'. However, the word 'gay' has a history of slang usage dating back to the eighteenth century and beyond, meaning prostitute, so the word has long had sexual connotations.

The history of gay identity is often dated to about 1869, when the word homosexuality was coined. The French theorist Michel Foucault argued that notions of personal identity have shifted from era to era and are expressions of power relationships. One group of people is tagged as abnormal to bolster the position of normal people – usually those in power. Around 1870, medical and scientific publications established the notion of a homosexual identity as a specific kind of personality, practice and case history. This is not to say that homosexual acts didn't happen before this date, but that after it this factor became the most important in establishing the identity of an individual. Homosexuality shifted from being a kind of behaviour to being a type of person.

This view can be challenged – there were homo-sexual subcultures at various earlier points in history, such as at the end of the sixteenth century and in the eighteenth – but has come to dominate this area of film studies. There is obviously nothing wrong with friendships between men but there may be a danger in automatically reading it as a sexual one. At the same time, there are hundreds of characters in films, whether or not identified as homosexual, who can be read as such.

This is still a problem today. In the film *The Adventures Of Priscilla, Queen Of The Desert* (1994) there is only one openly gay man, Adam, but even this is debatable. He combines a manly physique with an effeminate manner and ironically suggests that it's just a phase he's going through. At no point does he have sex with a man, nor is he intimate with another man. Tick, one of his travelling companions, is much less effeminate, although effeminacy in itself is not a defining characteristic of the male homosexual. The same lack of same-sex physical contact applies to him, plus he's married and has a son. Of course, homosexuals can marry and have children, but this should all be taken to show how difficult it is to define sexuality. Effeminacy, cross-dressing, particular walks and postures, a taste for show tunes and so on *can* be taken as signifiers of homosexuality, but not all homosexuals fit these stereotypes and not all who do are homosexual.

Homosociality And Fratriarchy

Culture is filled with relationships between men. Most films depict a male hero who goes into battle, literally or metaphorically, against a male villain, often with a male best friend at his side. Think of *Seven* (1995) – although best friend is overstating the relationship portrayed here. Relationships between people of the same sex have become known as 'homosociality'. Perhaps because of the interests of critics or the relative scarcity of examples, female homosociality is rarely examined; homosociality tends to be thought of as male bonding. Homosocial activities can include sexual behaviour but the term has tended to be restricted to platonic relationships.

Homosocial bonds between men of the same age, of the same peer group, constitute a 'fratriarchy'. This is a protective circle of friends who look out for each other, make use of each other and advise each other, whilst standing in a wary distrust of each other. Women stand outside this group as a threat to the unity of the masculine society and as a guarantee of the straightness of the individual. A good example of the fratriarchy might be found in *Jaws* (1975), in the uneasy alliance forged by Brody, Hooper and Quint in their search for the shark. There is a growing respect for each other, an attempt to support each other, especially after they have compared their various wounds. At the end of the film there is no reunion between Brody and his wife, as you might expect from Spielberg, since by then the heterosexual bond between them has been transcended or supplanted by the fratriarchy. The men have been tested and have passed. Fratriarchy can also be located in the friendship between Holden and Banky in *Chasing Amy* (1996); at the climax of the film Holden tries to rescue his relationship with the lesbian Alyssa by suggesting they all sleep together, in the process outing Banky.

Gays And Lesbians On Film

Given the available space, this is a brief history – Vito Russo's *Celluloid Closet* covers the period up to the mid-1980s but is stronger on gay than lesbian material. In parallel to my very broad outline there are various low-budget pictures worth attention – Jean Genet's *Un Chant D'Amour* (1950), Kenneth Anger's *Fireworks* (1947) and *Scorpio Rising* (1964), and the career of Derek Jarman from biopic *Sebastiane* (1976) to *Blue* (1993). There were few openly gay directors – James Whale and George Cukor being notable exceptions – until the 1990s and few openly gay actors, although a number have been outed posthumously, allowing for ironic re-readings of their oeuvres.

The history of the gay man on screen up to the 1940s is that of the sissy – the male weakling, the mother's boy. Two late examples of this can be found in *The Maltese Falcon* (1941), firstly in Peter Lorre's rather fey depiction of Joel Cairo. Even when he holds his gun at Spade he is a weakling and easily disarmed. Alongside him is the tough-talking but equally ineffectual and easily disarmed Wilmer. Wilmer is described as a gunsel – slang for homosexual – and there is some suggestion that he is Gutman's boy, though this may be Spade trying to rile them. In the aftermath of both world wars there was a retreat from showing male friendships in a way which might be misinterpreted and the Hays Code theoretically prevented such things even being hinted at.

From the 1940s until the 1970s gays were victims or villains. Hitchcock has depicted various murderous characters whose sexuality is at best ambiguous – Philip and

Brandon in *Rope* (1948), Bruno in *Strangers On A Train* (1951) and of course Norman Bates in *Psycho* (1960). This tradition continues right through to *Cruising* (1980) featuring a serial killer in the gay community and *Silence Of The Lambs* (1991) and *JFK* (1991). In counterpoint to this are *Tea And Sympathy* (1956), *Victim* (1961), *A Taste Of Honey* (1961) and *The Leather Boys* (1964), which were pleas for sympathy – sometimes as much for sissies. In *A Taste Of Honey* the homosexual character is exiled from the one happy place in his life, although this is an advance on the tendency for gay characters to commit suicide in despair at the end of a film.

In 1980s British cinema things improved. *My Beautiful Laundrette* (1986), directed by Stephen Frears from a Hanif Kureshi script, featured an interracial love affair between a skinhead and a Pakistani. This was a rare film in that the characters accepted their sexuality rather than being anxious about it – it was simply a given. The same director also made *Prick Up Your Ears* (1987), a biopic about gay playwright Joe Orton who was murdered by his lover. The Alan Bennett script was the first mainstream picture to show gay sex in public toilets. At the same period the fetish for adaptations of E M Forster led to a sumptuous treatment of his posthumously published novel *Maurice* (filmed 1987). Films about gay subjects were acceptable – if made by openly straight directors.

The AIDS crisis from the 1980s onwards restored the gay man's victim status. Early American depictions include *Parting Glances* (1985, featuring Steve Buscemi) and *Longtime Companion* (1990), but *Philadelphia* (1993) was the first Hollywood film on the subject. Tom Hanks's character barely even touched his screen lover, played by Antonio Banderas; you could play gay as long as there was no sex. Oscars all round, naturally.

The image of gay as victim and as killer was both exploded and reclaimed in a number of films released in the early 1990s. Tom Kalin's *Swoon* (1991) retold the Leopold and Loeb murder, first shown on screen in *Rope*. Richard Loeb had offered Nathan Leopold sex in return for his committing a series of crimes, up to and including murder, at a period when such sexuality was considered a crime in itself. The film is set in prohibition era Chicago and features an examination of racism and sexism alongside its frank depiction of Leopold's and Loeb's lives and deaths. Gregg Araki's *The Living End* (1992) offered an AIDS road movie, in which two HIV positive gay men go on the run, figuring they have nothing to lose as they are doomed to die anyway.

These films, along with others, became collectively known as New Queer Cinema. These were films made by openly gay film directors – Kalin, Araki, Isaac Julien, Todd Haynes (*Poison* (1990), *Velvet Goldmine* (1998), *Far From Heaven* (2002)) and in retrospect Derek Jarman – who refused either to apologise for their characters or see their homosexuality as a problem. Lesbian filmmakers had initially been part of the publicity machine for New Queer Cinema, but rapidly became sidelined. Meanwhile, its success allowed gay characters to appear in romantic comedies – such as *Four Weddings And A Funeral* (1993), *The Object Of My Affection* (1997) and *Happy Endings* (2005). *Brokeback Mountain* (2005) appeared to be a breakthrough mainstream drama with gay themes, but actually belongs to the tradition of gay gothic in which one of the lovers has to die.

The history of lesbian film is sketchier, which seems

in line with the comparative scarcity of films that are made by or about women. An important early example is *Mädchen In Uniform* (1931), about the romantic attachment which develops between a young girl and her teacher. The headmistress attacks their affair as scandalous but the pupils defend them. At the end of the film the young girl is prevented from committing suicide. In the United States the film was cut to keep the love affair as a crush.

These Three (1936) and its remake *The Children's Hour* (1962), both directed by William Wyler, are also school stories. A child accuses two teachers of having 'strange sexualities'. The earlier version actually depicts a heterosexual love triangle rather than a lesbian affair – the studio and the Hays Code ensuring that it was less explicit than its source play. The remake used the strange sexuality to titillate the audience in the publicity material, but the film was a flop. In *The Killing Of Sister George* (1968), Beryl Reid played a butch – that is masculine – lesbian and soap actress, who has been written out of a television series at the same time as she has lost her lover. Reid portrays an unacceptable face of lesbianism – out, and a frequenter of gay bars – and naturally her character is punished for it.

By the 1980s films began to feature characters who could be read as lesbians – Tony Scott's *The Hunger* (1983) is one of many films that uses lesbian imagery to explore ideas of vampirism, as Catherine Deneuve's ancient vampire seduces a doctor played by Susan Sarandon. Sarandon's character is promised eternal youth but death is her only option. Two years later Spielberg adapted Alice Walker's *The Color Purple* (1985), but in the process shifted clear lesbianism in the source novel to close female friendship between Celie (Whoopie Goldberg) and Shug, a blues singer. Similarly, *Fried Green Tomatoes At The Whistle Stop Café* (1991) offered the empowering relationship in the present day between two women, played by Jessica Tandy and Kathy Bates, remembering the past of the café which featured another friendship between women. Director Jon Avnet decided that it was better to avoid filming lesbianism for fear of alienating an audience, whilst leaving it as a subtext to be detected by those in the know.

More problematic is the sexually explicit *Bound* (1995), a variation on the money-in-a-suitcase thriller in which two women attempt to steal from Caesar (Joe Pantoliano). Violet (Jennifer Tilly) is portrayed as a blonde femme – the supposedly passive partner in a relationship – but is in fact the seducer of Corky (Gina Gershon) and the one finally in control. Corky is initially portrayed as butch, with a leather jacket, boots, trousers, tattoos and wielding a gun, but spends much of the film tied up and powerless. The film is unusual for its depiction of a sexual relationship between two women and undermines lesbian stereotypes, but at the same time the relationship may just titillate a male audience.

New Queer Cinema did feature some lesbian directors – Sandie Benning, Laurie Lynd, Su Friedrich, Monica Treut and Rose Troche – and in 1995 ten lesbian features were released in the United States. These features were narrative films, whereas most lesbian cinema had been experimental, documentary or short. Few openly lesbian directors have escaped from the ghetto of video and *avant-garde* filmmaking into making films with anything like a budget. Rose Troche eventually followed her *Go Fish* (1994) with a London-based romantic comedy, *Bedrooms And Hallways* (1998) and then *The Safety Of Objects* (2001). She has since worked more in television. There are few female directors, there are even fewer lesbian directors. The dominant film image of the lesbian remains Sharon Stone's murderous ice maiden in *Basic Instinct* (1992) – first claimed as homophobic and since reclaimed as empowering.

The Structure Of The Buddy Movie

As homosexuality has rarely been openly depicted in films, there has been a tendency for queer readings to identify hidden gays; ostensibly heterosexual characters are revealed to be homosexual. Robin Wood has shown sexual subtexts in films like *The Deer Hunter* (1978) and *Raging Bull* (1980). In his analysis of a series of buddy movies from the late 1960s and early 1970s – *Butch Cassidy And The Sundance Kid* (1969), *Easy Rider* (1969), *Midnight Cowboy* (1969), *Thunderbolt And Lightfoot* (1974) – he identifies six areas of gay romance: 1) the journey with no authentic goal; 2) the marginalisation of women; 3) the lack of a home; 4) the male love story; 5) an explicit homosexual character; and 6) death of one or both of the central characters.

The same structure can be found in *Gattaca* (1997), where in a genetically perfect future the natural-born Vincent (Ethan Hawke) borrows the DNA of the crippled Jerome (Jude Law) to pass as a trainee astronaut. When the director of the Gattaca Institute is murdered, Vincent fears exposure and discovers one of the detectives on the case is his brother. The journey is the space mission which Vincent desires – here a McGuffin to set the plot in action, and not engaged upon until the end of the film. Women are certainly marginalised; a girlfriend (Uma Thurman) with little to do in the plot, a mother seen only at the start, a few nurses. Vincent and Jerome have both left their homes behind and uneasily cohabit in a place which looks more like a lab than somewhere to live. But their relationship, their fratriarchy, is central to the film, as they have to cover for each other and share the girlfriend to escape detection. The appearance of Gore Vidal – an openly gay writer and occasional actor – can be thought of as representing what 'true' homosexuality is, thereby throwing suspicion off the Vincent/Jerome relationship. It seems an inexplicable piece of casting unless such a reading is intended. Finally, Jerome kills himself as Vincent leaves Earth, having given him a lock of hair in much the same way as a maid might give a keepsake to her knight who is leaving for the crusades.

Almost any buddy or mismatched cop movie could be queered, from *Lethal Weapon* (1987) to *Seven* (1995) and beyond. In a romantic comedy it is obvious that any male and female who are arguing will be married by the end of the film. When two men argue in precisely the same way... well, Hollywood dare not depict it (although *Kiss Kiss Bang Bang* (2005), directed by Shane Black the author of the *Lethal Weapon* films, at least plays with the idea.

Camp

One version of a gay or queer aesthetic is camp. Perhaps the most influential thinker on the subject of camp is Susan Sontag (1933–2004), in her 'Notes On Camp', although in the process she attempts to 'de-gay' camp, so that heterosexuals can engage in it too. Camp is the sense of excess – whether it is an excess of stylisation or of colour (see *Priscilla*) – a sense of irony with life lived in quotation marks or an attempt to see the world through the eyes of a dandy as a lived performance. Camp comes in two kinds: deliberate and unintended.

Mike Hodges's version of *Flash Gordon* (1980) offers the first, with its nostalgic special effects mimicking Saturday morning serials, its fetishisation of Flash's skimpy shorts and even the use of Queen on the soundtrack. In many ways this form of camp has come to be a dominant mode of film since the mid-1990s, especially in much of Australia's films, in particular Baz Luhrmann's, and in openly gay movies such as those made by Todd Haynes.

Unintended camp arises when the filmmakers have become too serious, or are unaware of the ludicrousness of their material – Dr Pretorius in *The Bride Of Frankenstein* (1935), some of the behaviour of Humphrey Bogart's characters in *The Maltese Falcon* and *The Big Sleep* (1946), and *The Sound Of Music* (1965), especially in its sing-along incarnation. This kind of campness is an audience appropriation of the film for its own amusement. In some of these cases it isn't clear that directors, producers and actors weren't setting out to make a camp movie in the first place.

Gay audiences can use camp to identify gay rôle models, albeit ironised rôle models, within otherwise entirely straight films. In the long decades when every gay man on screen was a victim or a psychopath, it provided a series of powerful figures who were neither, or were a better class of psychopath. The explosion of camp – especially in our obsession with big-screen remakes of half-forgotten 1960s and 1970s television series – might be seen as the sudden release of creative tension after a century of cinema censorship. At the same time, to assume camp is the only gay identity, or the only aesthetic, is to risk a potentially homophobic stereotyping, as is any attempt to entirely de-gay camp.

Chapter 9

Stars

Important though *auteur* theory is, and fascinating as Marxism, semiotics, feminism and psychoanalysis may be, they're not the reasons most of us go to the movies. Whilst there are a few big names that register with the general public – Woody Allen, George Lucas, Steven Spielberg, at a push James Cameron – we are more likely to part with our money to see Samuel L. Jackson, Kevin Spacey, Cameron Diaz or Cate Blanchett. Whilst the French critics of the 1950s period *Cahiers Du Cinéma* may have waxed lyrical over Humphrey Bogart or Marlon Brando, that wasn't where their hearts were. Laura Mulvey may have talked about audience identification with male stars, but this was more an analysis of the mechanics of cinema than an homage to an actor. It was not until the late 1970s that critics began to take stars seriously. This analysis comes from two major, overlapping, directions: study of production and study of consumption.

Production

You don't get to be Ben Affleck or Jennifer Lopez on sheer talent alone (and the films these two have made since the first two editions of this book prove this). The late, great J T Walsh stole dozens of movies from under the noses of bigger stars (go see him act Nicholas Cage and Dennis Hopper off the screen in *Red Rock West* (1992) for a start) but didn't become a star. Steve Buscemi has a score or more of memorable cameos in quirky movies, has directed films and tv episodes, but he's still not a star. Stars are created by various aspects of the media, and can be seen as aspects of the production of capital – whether purely as a monetary asset or as cultural capital. Richard Dyer lists four areas of this production in his book *Stars*: promotion, publicity, films and criticism/commentaries.

Promotion is the work done by the studio to put a particular image across of their star actors – and in the days of the studio system they could virtually recreate an actor's life from scratch into something suitable for their publicity. The wrong country of origin could be changed, an unfortunate name (Archibald Leach, William Henry Pratt) could be altered, and if the star was a homosexual a girlfriend could be provided. The studio controlled almost every aspect of their actors' lives, and decided which films they could or must appear in. Warner Brothers had one set of actors, MGM another and so on.

The studios would release carefully tailored biographical information to the press, especially to reviewers at press screenings, schedule appearances at premieres, organise interviews and license pin-ups and endorsements of particular products. All of this would be done with the aim of fostering a particular image of a given star – whether dangerous glamour girl or debonair man about town. Perhaps the most sustained acting that some stars did was as themselves – for example, Cary

Grant is usually cited as playing himself in his films.

In addition there is more obvious advertising – the trailer, the poster, the advertising hoarding. Whether the name is above or below the title, whether it is on the left- or right-hand side of the rectangular hoarding, or whether it is at the end of a list and labelled 'and —' says something about the status of an actor. The latter category should also say 'cameo appearance' to the audience, though Ben Affleck appears in rather too much of the abysmal *Phantoms* (1998) than is suggested by his 'and Ben Affleck' credit. The progress of Affleck's career might be tracked by his non-appearance on the cover of the video version of *Mallrats* (1995) to being on some versions of the cover (*sans* beard, unlike in the film itself) of *Chasing Amy* (1996) and first in an alphabetical list on *Dogma* (1999). By the time he gets to star in *Pearl Harbor* (2001) his name is above the title on the cover, his face coming between Kate Beckinsale and Josh Hartnett – by then, post-*Good Will Hunting* (1997) and *Armageddon* (1998), he can clearly be used to sell a film. (Post *Gigli* (2003), on the other hand …)

Affleck is a product of a post-Classical Hollywood era. With the breakdown of the studio system in the sense of there being stables of actors, the publicity machine has become more diffuse. Studios still arrange scores of meet-the-press interviews to market their product, with their actors being asked the same few basic questions and giving the same basic answers. Fan clubs and fanzines, once likely to be controlled by studios, are now joined by official websites with their potted lists of previous appearances.

The distinction between all this and publicity is that the former is deliberate. In publicity – with the dictum in mind that there is no such thing as bad publicity – things about the actors are 'discovered' by the press or the interviewee lets something slip. This might be some juicy details about whom they are seeing this year, their battle with drink or drugs, or embarrassing encounters with hookers. The sexuality of actors such as Kevin Spacey and Keanu Reeves has been the hook for pointless speculation, and Hugh Grant's arrest sold warehouses full of tabloids. The truly juicy scandal – a rape or murder charge – is relatively rare and would probably finish a career, but tales of drug use or infidelity can actually add to a star's image.

And then there are the films themselves – the lifeblood of the actor. In the past, the studio would decide the type of film that an actor would appear in. Humphrey Bogart tended to play gangsters in the 1930s, but from the 1940s he played hard-drinking lone detectives. Bogart's transition came with the success of *The Maltese Falcon* (1941) and *Casablanca* (1942), and in neither case was he first choice for the rôle. Bogart's characters would be tough, on the edge of the law, but probably have a heart of gold underneath it all and would be balanced by a seemingly vulnerable woman who might turn out to be tough and duplicitous after all. (And in the background would be the public's image of his relationship with Lauren Bacall, forged on the set of *To Have And Have Not* (1945), Bacall being a star created by director Howard Hawks.)

The career of Harrison Ford offers a more recent example. In the early years, with Han Solo of the *Star Wars* trilogy and Rick Deckard of *Blade Runner* (1982), Ford's characters offered some degree of moral complexity – the mercenary, the near rapist. Through the 1980s and into the 1990s, though, Ford's characters turned up the decency. Indiana Jones may display the attitudes to race and gender of the 1930s, but he is basically a decent man and his quest for treasures is to enrich museums rather than himself (although the ethics of museums having them is never questioned). In films like *Witness* (1985) and *Working Girl* (1988), his characters maintain their moral code or even have it enhanced by their experiences. Most problematically, in *Regarding Henry* (1991), a workaholic is turned into the perfect family man by being shot in the head. Given this run of performances – some might say typecasting – it then comes as a surprise, if not necessarily as a relief, to see him in *What Lies Beneath* (2000). At first sight he appears to be a caring lover, but as the film progresses a murky past comes back to haunt him and his co-star. More recently he has been playing fathers or father figures.

Dyer suggests that stars may be cast for a selective fit for a rôle, a perfect fit and a problematic fit. In the selective fit some aspects of their star persona are being used, and others downplayed – think of the basically decent side to Nicholas Cage in *Raising Arizona* (1987), *Red Rock West* or *8mm* (1998), as opposed to the crazy, arm-raising character seen in *Wild At Heart* (1990) or *Snake Eyes* (1998). The perfect fit, on the other hand, is often a star vehicle written with an actor in mind or tailored to his or her strengths after casting. Think of the various Steve Martin comedies, or the various personae of Woody Allen in his own films. The final category comes when the actor is cast against type or is the wrong shape for an already familiar rôle. Sometimes the tensions will override the performance, sometimes the character will be compromised – an actor known for playing heroes may insist on the redemption of a villain if they play one – or the star's image will shine through and be accepted by the audience, irrespective of the suitability of their casting. Dyer's example is Marilyn Monroe as Lorelei in *Gentlemen Prefer Blondes* (1953), a cynical manipulative character in the original novel by Anita Loos and in a Broadway musical that had starred Carol Channing – whereas Marilyn Monroe was perceived as the innocent abroad.

Finally there is the category of criticism/commentaries, which can range from reviews in the local newspaper to learned Ph.Ds and Pocket Essentials on particular actors. This might be a positive appreciation of their efforts or a revisionist damning of their overacting. It includes articles, interviews, profiles and other forms of analysis, and may be written during the lifetime of the actor in question or after his or her death. In a kind of metacommentary, this material may also include analysis of the promotion, publicity and films of an actor, as well as a dialogue with earlier criticism. The examination of the nature of the star is part of the stardom.

A number of actors have been singled out for such attention – Grant for his string of successes in the 1930s, 1950s and 1960s, John Wayne for his exploration of a certain kind of rugged masculinity, James Dean and Monroe for the brevity of their lives and so forth. The heart-throb of the month – Matt Damon, Josh Hartnett, Ryan Gosling, Leonardo who? – often becomes the subject of a cut-and-paste biography, filled out with paparazzi shots, to cash in on a fleeting star status.

What Dyer is keen to point out is that stars do not have a single, fixed, unitary status. Grant's persona contains both the debonair gentleman and the nervous bachelor, with an alarming tendency to cross-dress. Performances shift in significance with the benefit of hindsight – Dean's anxious teen in *Rebel Without A Cause* (1955) or *East Of Eden* (1955), especially the scenes of his driving a car, takes on a different dimension with knowledge of his subsequent death. Speculation about his sexuality perhaps revises the way we think about his character's relationship with Plato. A star may be uncovered from the archives, re-evaluated as underrated, or knocked down for overacting.

To think of this from a semiotic angle, the star is a collection of signifiers which point to a series of signifieds. At different times different signifiers are thought to be dominant, or a particular era will privilege one set of connotations over another. An 'innocent' audience of the 1950s would view the Doris Day/Rock Hudson relationship in films such as *Pillow Talk* (1959), *Lover Come Back* (1961) and *Send No Flowers* (1964), rather differently from the post-1980s audience which knows Hudson died of an AIDS-related illness. The temptation to go back and search through those films for evidence of his sexuality is now almost impossible to resist – the signifiers must have been there but not correctly interpreted.

Consumption

Mulvey's 'Visual Pleasure And Narrative Cinema' assumes a context of psychoanalysis, in particular that of a Freudian/Lacanian position. She assumes that there are two kinds of gaze: an identificatory gaze at the male hero and a desiring one at the female love interest.

Whilst there is a lot of mileage within this, there are clearly problems here. For a start, there is the assumption of a universal audience position – certainly male and heterosexual, and probably white and middle class. The female spectator has to cross-dress and become a male. Clearly sexuality, race, sex and class will have an impact upon the way we identify with characters or feel excluded from empathy, and whom we desire on screen.

Jackie Stacey offers an alternate way of viewing female spectatorship that is more complex than simply reversing Mulvey's ideas to assume identification with the female characters and desire for the male characters. In the process of writing her book *Stargazing*, she researched the feelings that British women had for American female stars of the 1940s and 1950s, as expressed in fan letters, membership of fan clubs, or questionnaires and surveys. Stacey divides audience reactions into two broad types: within and outside the cinema.

This appreciation within the context of watching a film in a cinema might be shown in the form of devotion from a distance, an unalloyed appreciation of the female star's appearance and actions, which need not be considered as sexual. The stars were out of reach, unobtainable, other-worldly and the object of veneration. In other cases the spectator may wish to become someone like the star – in hairstyle, costume, behaviour. The star was a rôle model to emulate. Related to this was an admiration for the actions of female stars, both on and off camera, with their power being envied. Doris Day and Katharine Hepburn's ability to have a career and to hold their own in a string of comedies was admired;

stars like Sharon Stone and Sandra Bullock might be the current equivalent. Such beauty, intelligence and power offer a fantasy of escape for the viewer, beyond the dreary everyday world of the patriarchy. It might be accepted that the female viewer could not become Bette Davis or Rita Hayworth, but for an hour or so in the darkness of a cinema theatre they could be them.

Outside the cinema there is a whole series of transformations the individual might undergo to show his or her relation to the star. The first version Stacey outlines is pretending: in children's games playing at being Bette Davis or Paltrow, or claiming some distant biological relationship to the famous. Secondly, there is the perception of the way in which the star resembles the individual – whether it is hair colour or a particular kind of stare, and so some sense of commonality is established between the viewer and the star. If a resemblance cannot be established, then imitation might be attempted: the voice of Monroe, the particular walk of Joan Crawford, or the way a cigarette could be lit or inhaled. Such imitations were temporary actions but in more extreme cases – although most common – the female audience member would attempt to copy the star, whether by adopting the star's hairstyle or dressing like them. Naturally this involves financial outlay, whether paying a hairdresser or buying shoes and clothes. This last form of identification involves economic consumption and the circulation of capital.

In both Dyer's and Stacey's analysis of stardom, the making of money is central. For Dyer the various manifestations of stardom are ways for the media – film studios, film companies and various advertisers and newspapers – to make money from a set of products:

Affleck, Lopez, Monroe, Bogart. In Stacey's model, which could equally well be applied to an analysis of male stars, there is a more disparate circulation of capital, like that on clothing and beauty products. Whilst the films can be analysed to interpret each star's position as a corporate asset and what ideological work their image performs, we do not get an analysis of the real Affleck or Lopez. Even the most intimate portrayal or open interview simply modifies the star's image and potential for making money.

Chapter 10

Genres

What Is Genre?

It might be argued that there are only three genres: documentary, fiction and *avant-garde*. These three genres might be distinguished by their attitude to the depiction of reality or their quest for artistic expression. The first films were in a sense documentaries – the arrival of a train. But as soon as events became staged, notions of fiction and narrative began to dominate. The *avant-garde* film attempts to depict a truth that isn't purely documentary, nor can it necessarily be reached by narratives.

Within these three genres – or, better, modes – there are identifiable classes of films which can be labelled as genres. Just as there are different kinds of documentary – fly-on-the-wall, talking head, docusoap, reality show and so forth – so there are different kinds of fiction. The idea of genre is not unique to film and can be found in other cultural products.

For our purposes it is worth beginning to think of genre as a group of films among which can be identified a recognisable series of conventions for characters, plots, locations, audience responses, *mises en scène*, themes and structures. This becomes a bit worrying, because *auteur* theory and theories of authorship tend to identify a series of films with a similar shopping list. Whilst a genre might be exploited by a single director, normally several work within it.

Genre theory has developed since the 1970s as a counterbalance to *auteur* theory. Within traditional literary criticism, genres, or at least popular genres such as science fiction, fantasy, horror and romance, tended to be looked down upon. A similar pattern occurs in film studies, where individual *auteurs* are celebrated but genre is dismissed as the product of hacks or *metteurs en scène*. Even those directors who do work within genres – such as Alfred Hitchcock – are thought to transcend their genres.

However, it could be argued that the history of Hollywood is the history of genres, and some genres are acceptable: Westerns and gangster films for their places within American myth-making, melodrama for its part in feminism and horror for its place in psychoanalytic discourse. Science fiction cinema came of age with postmodernism; other genres find champions. But how do you define an individual genre?

The Problem Of Genre

Take *Metropolis* (1926), *The Day The Earth Stood Still* (1951), *Alphaville* (1965), *2001: A Space Odyssey* (1968), *Star Wars* (1977) and *Gattaca* (1997). There should be no difficulty in recognising this as a list of science fiction films – but what do they have in common? Science fiction might be set in the future, but *The Day The Earth Stood Still* is set contemporaneously and *Star Wars* is either set in the past or uses the idea of a past. Sf includes spaceships – ignoring *Metropolis* and *Alphaville* – or aliens – ignoring *Gattaca*. Sf is a series of narratives about the interaction of humanity and technology – except that this would then require us to consider *Apollo 13* (1995) and *The Dish* (2001) as science fiction.

Several of these films are other things as well: *Metropolis* is a dystopia, *The Day The Earth Stood Still* a cold war thriller/parable, *Star Wars* by turns a Western, a comedy or a war movie and *Gattaca* a murder mystery. Many sf films can also be thought of as horror, from the Universal films of the 1930s through 1950s monster movies, *Alien* (1979) and *Pitch Black* (2000) and beyond.

We anticipate different aspects of individual films: characters, plots, locations, audience responses, *mises en scène*, themes and structures. A film with cowboys and Indians is a Western; with a detective and criminals it is crime; with gangsters (surprisingly) it is a gangster flick, and so on. One in which a crime is committed and then solved is also a crime movie, one in which obstacles postpone the love between two characters is a romance. Films set in Monument Valley are Westerns, those set in space (excluding *Apollo 13*) are science fiction. If the audience laughs, it is a comedy; if they scream, it is horror. If the film features dark shadows and odd camera angles, then it is likely to be a *film noir*.

But structures can be problematic because they are replicated from genre to genre. *Ten Little Indians* (1965), *Halloween* (1978), *Alien* and *Pitch Black* each feature narratives where a group of characters are killed off one by one; *Alien* is country house murder enacted on a spaceship (and *The Thing* (1982) does it at an Antarctic base), or a haunted house in outer space (ditto).

Underlying almost all plots is the structure equilibrium, disaster, chaos, restoration or new equilibrium – whether *Casablanca* (1942) or *Reservoir Dogs* (1991). When a film does not follow this structure, the tension created by its divergence is often the point.

This pattern echoes the master narrative of status quo/chaos/new status quo described by structuralist Tzvetan Todorov and may also be found in crime thrillers. First a normal, if idyllic, community is established, before something comes into the community to shatter the piece. One or two heroes (and often a heroine) come together to fight back and defeat the evil, restoring normality or creating a new society. In prologues – sometimes at the start of the movie, even pre-credits – an original murder or trauma is shown as the root cause of the chaos. In *Halloween* it is Michael Myers's murder of his sister, before the action cuts to fifteen years later; *Friday the 13th* (1980) and *A Nightmare On Elm Street* (1984) imply such an event. The (optional) epilogue reveals the villain isn't dead after all (*Halloween*), and even has him coming back to try to kill the heroine (*I Know What You Did Last Summer* (1997)).

Similar structures can occur in crime thrillers: an initial crime, or the origin of the criminal, the everyday world of the detective, the discovery of a pattern of crimes, progress towards solving the crime and restoring order, and then, sometimes, a twist in the tale. *Seven* (1995) broadly fits this pattern, as does *Blue Steel* (1989), which slightly distorts the order: the convenience store robbery in which the villain gains a gun, Jamie Lee Curtis's career as a rookie cop, the series of murders which she helps to solve, and then the final proof of the villain's guilt. Crime and horror films both deal with the breaking of laws – whether laws of criminality or nature.

Equally, a film may use a generic element, without joining that genre. The majority of films have some element of romance, without that ever becoming central to the narrative. On the other hand, sometimes peripheral elements define a genre. Take the war movie genre. *Casablanca* is set during wartime, is located in occupied French territory, has Nazis as villains and ends with characters either escaping to then neutral territory or going to join the Resistance, but otherwise does not depict fighting. Whilst the narrative could omit the Second World War (see *Barb Wire* (1995)), it nevertheless needs to be considered a war movie, if only for its anti-isolationist propaganda directed at an America that had not yet joined the war. Vietnam War movies rarely depict conflict – in *The Deer Hunter* (1978) it only takes up a few seconds of screen time. *Apocalypse Now* (1979) and *Casualties Of War* (1989) focus on a group of men and offer narratives that would fit in any war.

Modelling Genres

Rick Altman offers a model of genres that draws on structuralism: genres are semantic or syntactic. In semantic genres we expect a certain number of elements: a Wild West town, a sheriff, good and bad cowboys, raiding Indians, deserts, six-guns and horses. Once this set of criteria is fulfilled, then the genre is defined as, say, a Western. On the other hand, a syntactic genre is one in which a certain narrative structure is expected, for example a film in which a woman meets a man she doesn't like but eventually falls in love with is a romantic comedy.

Unfortunately, we might feel that we could describe a film as being both part of a semantic genre or of a syntactic genre. Westerns often have an element of the revenge plot about them, whether it is John Wayne as the uncle tracking down his kidnapped niece and seeking revenge on the Indians, or feuding families in various versions of the Wyatt Earp and OK Corral story or *High Noon* (1952), whilst still fulfilling the semantic criteria for Westerns.

The History Of Genres

Each genre has its own history – and arguably every genre follows that history, although it may take different lengths of time to go through each stage. Before a genre is born, there are films which (in retrospect) belong to that genre. In retrospect, both *Psycho* (1960) and *Peeping Tom* (1960) can be seen as slasher movies, where a male character (Norman Bates in *Psycho*, Mark Lewis in *Peeping Tom*) stabs a series of women to death before being caught or killed. Both broke new boundaries in taste and decency for their time, and both may be considered as black comedies or films about voyeurism. Further films were made about such murderers, such as *The Texas Chain Saw Massacre* (1974) and some of Dario Argento's films, such as *Suspiria* (1976), but it was only with *Halloween* that a genre came into being. (Mark Whitehead's Pocket Essentials on *Slasher Movies* admirably charts this territory.)

In *Halloween* all the elements of the slasher movie are in place: the prologue charting the origin of the psycho-killer, and then the main event, in a particular time or place, in which the killer goes around picking characters off one by one. These characters are curiously isolated – with the police absent, disbelieving or helpless – and aren't initially aware of what is happening to their peers. There's a pattern to the victims: anyone who has had sex is fair game, as are people who smoke or drink. Anyone separated from the others is also dead meat. Finally there are just one or two victims left, usually a virtuous female (a clean-living virgin) who makes a last stand and appears to defeat the killer, although often it's revealed that she has the wrong man, or that he hasn't died after all (cue sequel ...).

Not only did *Halloween* spawn many follow-ups, but other films began to exploit the pattern. The revenge of (actually on behalf of) a drowned boy at a school camp leads to multiple murders in *Friday The 13th* and many sequels, alongside numerous stand-alone movies such *Prom Night* (1980), where avenging a murdered sister provides the impetus for the plot. Both the directors and the audiences know what is expected: people have to be killed in increasingly graphic ways, the audience needs to be titillated, and the next scare encourages audience members to turn for reassurance to their partners. *A Nightmare On Elm Street* (1984) and its sequels took the inventiveness to new heights (and depths). These featured the continued revenge of Freddy Krueger, a child molester who had been burnt by the angry population of Elm Street.

The central rôle of female protagonists in many of these films – often played by Jamie Lee Curtis, the daughter of Janet Leigh who had played *ur*-victim

Marion Crane in *Psycho* – and the films' incredible popularity with males under 25 led Carol J Clover to suggest that here we have the unusual phenomenon of males identifying with a woman. Clover's *Men, Women And Chainsaws* remains very readable and is very informative. Equally, young men may like watching young women being stalked and menaced, and the many point-of-view shots encourage their identification with the villain rather than the victim. The increasing use of witty one-liners by Freddy Krueger echoed the dialogue of action heroes such as Arnold Schwarzenegger and Bruce Willis in countless movies in the 1980s and 1990s, as the original killer Terminator mutates into a perfect father and Krueger's knife glove (available at a toy shop near you) metamorphosed into the loveable and tragic *Edward Scissorhands* (1990).

The slasher conventions began to seep into films that were not part of the genre. *Alien* (1979) is an early example that transposes the villain to an alien, the unreachable place to outer space and the final girl to Ripley, but the narrative pattern remains the same. *The Terminator* (1984) has a time-travelling cyborg villain, tracking down final girl Sarah Connor. Avenging women are at the heart of films such as *Fatal Attraction* (1987), in which the foolish actions of a straying husband lead to attempts to kill him or his wife, before a set-piece showdown between the threesome. *What Lies Beneath* (2000) adds a ghost story to the suspicions of a betrayed wife.

After the best part of two decades, the genre began to look a bit tired, but new attempts to resuscitate it appeared, ironically from one of the more successful directors to have jumped upon the bandwagon. Just as

Friday The 13th had reinvented itself, so *Wes Craven's New Nightmare* (1994) saw a conscious revival of a franchise and Craven's return to directing Krueger, as well as the appearance on screen of Craven, Heather Langenkamp and Robert Englund, playing 'themselves'. Craven confronted the cheapening of the franchise and the dilution of his original concept, as well as examining the boundary between reality and the imagination. Too clever for its own good, the film was not particularly well received, but it made *Scream* (1996) possible.

Kevin Williamson's script for *Scream* features characters who know about slasher movies, know the rules that state who dies, yet still die one by one. The film's success logically led to *Scream 2* (1997), featuring the survivors and new characters a few years later, where a copycat is stalking the survivors and a film of the earlier events is in production. The increased self-referentiality includes debates on the merits of sequels, as a bloodier body count mounts. In time we had *Scream 3* (2000), without the creative input of Kevin Williamson, just as John Carpenter (*Halloween*), Sean S Cunningham (*Friday The 13th*) and Craven had moved away from their respective franchises. Like *New Nightmare* the setting is a studio, as another film is made. The rules of the slasher are outlined for us as we revisit the events of the original murders and discover more about what really happened. *Scream 3* claims to conclude the trilogy but slasher cycles have been resurrected before, with or without the original creative talent.

Alongside such revisionist slashers, straightforward parodies appeared. *Scary Movie* (2001) added little that *Scream 2*'s commentary on the racist nature of some slashers hadn't already said. After all, *Scary Movie* was a parody of a parody. *Shriek If You Know What I Did Last Friday The 13th* (2000) smacked of desperation. Despite the revisionism and the parody, the slasher movie seems to show no signs of dying as other genres have before it. *I Know What You Did Last Summer* was sold on Kevin Williamson's script and rather ignored the Lois Duncan novel it was loosely based on. This was an unashamed exercise in by-the-numbers plotting, with a cynical opening for a sequel ignored by the inevitable *I Still Know What You Did Last Summer* (1998). At a stretch the two films might be redeemed by their commentary on 1990s American class politics. *Cherry Falls* (2000) reversed the clichés by putting virgins at risk and *Urban Legend* (1998) borrowed actor Robert Englund to confuse matters as a series of murders is committed in homage to urban legends.

Whereas *Halloween* and *A Nightmare On Elm Street* featured largely unknown casts, by the late 1990s the teens were already stars or were cutting their teeth on television acting in *Dawson's Creek, Friends, Buffy The Vampire Slayer* or *Party Of Five*: Joshua Jackson, Sarah Michelle Gellar, Jennifer Love Hewitt as well as Freddy Prinze Jr and Ryan Phillipe. It was a brave or foolish screenwriter or director who chose to knife their characters. In this respect Gellar was unlucky; in Sunnydale she was the final girl kicking vampire butt (and demon butt, and robot or cyborg butt and ...), but she bit the dust in *Scream 2* and *I Know What You Did Last Summer*. Careless. The actors of the film-within-the-film of *Scream 3* may be cursing their agents for allowing them to appear in tosh like *Stab 3*, but the same doesn't seem to be true of the latest generation of Hollywood teens/twenty-somethings.

The genre continues with various remakes – Gus Van Sant's shot-for-shot copy of *Psycho* (1998) cast Anne Heche as Marion Crane. The actor was also familiar as the potential psycho from *I Know What You Did Last Summer*. Unbelievably, the remade *The Texas Chainsaw Massacre* (2003) made its original look subtle, and featured Eric Balfour, familiar from *Buffy*, *24*, *Six Feet Under*, *The OC* and dozens of other tv shows.

The history of individual genres is the history of film itself, in the way they interrelate to each other, in the way audience anticipations change and in the way that stars partake or reject such products. Almost as much as a given star, and in most cases more than a name director, for most cinema-goers genre is the key to knowing what to see on a Friday or Saturday night down at the multiplex, whether it be slasher, chick flick, romantic comedy or science fiction epic. Whilst the fortunes of individual genres wax and wane, it seems unlikely that genre will ever be abandoned altogether.

After two more fairly pointless *Halloween* sequels attempted to resuscitate the franchise – *Halloween H20: 20 Years Later* (1998, bringing back Jamie Lee Curtis's character and adding Josh Hartnett) and *Halloween: Resurrection* (2002, with Curtis but not Hartnett) – *Halloween* was remade in 2007 by Rob Zombie, the latest desecration of John Carpenter's back catalogue.

Chapter 11

National Cinema

The Nature Of National Cinema

There's an understandable tendency to think of Hollywood when thinking of film – old Tinseltown is clearly the centre of the filmmaking world in terms of world dominance, and surely more money is spent there than anywhere else. At cinemas in Britain most films shown are American. Partially this is sheer numbers – more films are made in the US than in Britain – but as well as production, it is also to do with the economics of distribution, that is, who distributes the films, and who shows them.

In a Hollywood film the language used is likely to be English, the camerawork, dubbing and other production values will at least be adequate, and it's unlikely to really challenge the viewer or make them suffer for their art (but see comments on recent Spielberg films in earlier chapters). Indeed art, aesthetics, might not even come into it – we are being sold a fairground ride with someone pretty to look at or identify with for 90 minutes or so. Thus far in this book the films I've looked at have been either made in Hollywood, or have been on the edges of Hollywood in the increasingly misnamed category of independent cinema. We mustn't ignore the films made in countries all over the world.

With much of this output there is a language barrier that can be partially crossed by using subtitles. Sometimes the production values are not what we are used to in Hollywood product. And films can depict cultural practices and share cultural assumptions that we are not familiar with. Rather than reject this material sight unseen, any difficulties should be embraced; anyone who limits themselves to Hollywood products is literally missing out on a world of wonders. The worldwide success of *Crouching Tiger, Hidden Dragon* (2000) obscures scores of (frankly much more interesting) Hong Kong films which don't necessarily have to involve Jackie Chan. India – best known for Bollywood films – actually produces more films than Hollywood, although comparatively few make it to the West. Films are made throughout Europe, and Latin America is fertile ground for investigation. Then there is English language film, from Britain, obviously, but also from Ireland, Canada (which also has Francophone films), New Zealand and, most importantly for this chapter, Australia.

National Cinema is, at its simplest, the cinematic product of a given country. Of course, in a few paragraphs' time I'm going to say that it isn't quite that easy, but for now let's maintain the illusion. Under this definition, Hollywood is itself a national cinema, the nation in this case being the United States of America. In film studies, National Cinema should be the label given to the study of films from a given country which pays particular attention to the production context (funding bodies and production facilities) and distribution networks that allow those films to be exhibited.

126

Additionally, these films are studied for the way they display, critique or create a sense of national identity. National identity is the set of characteristics held in common by citizens of a particular country, or those characteristics which are recognised as such by the community. Identity is created or recognised through language, stories, ideologies and myths, and can be used by the dominant members of a national power structure to justify their own position as rightful rulers. These characteristics may be thought of as constituting a stereotype, or more charitably an archetype; at the same time they are not just imposed by the state. They can be created, recognised or challenged by the individual: to depict a national stereotype may be as much to hold it up to ridicule as to engage in an act of patriotism.

Just as the national characteristics vary between countries, so do the contexts of production. Because the creation of a national character is in the interests of state, either for ruling its citizens at home or exporting a product (material or ideological or both) abroad, in many countries the government has input into the film industry. This might be tax breaks for investment, quotas of how much domestic product must be shown at cinemas or on television, or actual investment or subsidy via Arts Councils and Film Commissions. When money is invested, it comes with strings attached, such as the choice of actor (usually someone from the paying country), technicians or facilities. The money might be given to a director and producer who have come together for a particular project in isolation, or it might be within some kind of studio context.

Once the film is completed, it needs to be shown –

but there is no guarantee that it will be. In Britain many more films are made than shown and so hundreds of films languish in distribution limbo. There is the film festival circuit, of which Cannes is the most prominent but there are also festivals in London, Berlin, Venice, Melbourne and, king of the independent film circuit, the Sundance Institute Festival established by Robert Redford. An audience or jury prize is one way to aid the gaining of distribution contracts, but often the event is a space for launching a deal rather than closing one. In any case, the festival is not sufficient in itself to make a film commercially successful, though the publicity gained is invaluable. Because there is no guarantee of international success, the producer has to aim to make most money back in the domestic market.

The actuality doesn't always match the theory. Mike Hodges's film *Croupier* (1997), featuring Clive Owen as a wannabe writer who gains work at a casino, sank without trace on first release in Britain; as one of the few people who saw it (at a festival) I think this was unfair. Although it was no *Get Carter* (1971) or *Flash Gordon* (1980), it deserved an airing. It only got a slightly wider distribution in Britain after it became an unexpected hit in America. In the reverse situation, US-made films such as *Memento* (2000) and *O Brother, Where Art Thou?* (2000) were first exhibited in Britain before gaining an American release.

Another source of income is television and video cassette/DVD rights. The French cable television company Canal Plus is a frequent investor both in French films and films from across Europe, as well as in some of the more independently-minded American directors. Within Britain the establishment of Channel

4 as a minority interests channel led to funding for film production in return for screening rights. Unfortunately, the loss of relatively small sums of money by the production wing FilmFour and a down-turn in advertising revenue seems likely to curtail its participation in production and distribution for the foreseeable future. The BBC also ventures from time to time into funding feature films, although initially these films could only be shown cinematically outside of Britain, in part because of rights agreements negotiated with acting and technicians' unions, and in part to maximise viewers for the television premiere.

Directors of less commercial films may find them-selves having to attract funding from several such bodies, from several countries, each with their own demands. A Peter Greenaway movie such as *The Baby Of Mâcon* (1993) had to look for money from The Netherlands, France and Germany along with British funds. Is it a British film? Then there's an Australian film like *The Piano* (1993), which was directed by Jane Campion, a New Zealander, is set in Scotland and New Zealand and stars two Americans – Harvey Keitel and Holly Hunter. I said it would get more complicated.

More examples: the Canadian director Atom Egoyan's *Felicia's Journey* (1999), shot in Birmingham, UK, is a US/Canadian co-production, *Dark City* (1997) and *The Matrix* (1999) are both Hollywood films shot in Australian-based studios owned by American corpo-rations – except of course that it depends what you mean by American. Twentieth-Century Fox is part of Australian Rupert Murdoch's empire, and ownership of other studios can probably be traced to Japanese and other Far Eastern financiers. *Dark City* and *The Matrix* were presumably made with an eye on the American market, as was *Moulin Rouge* (2001 – set in France, shot in Australia, directed by an Australian, starring an Australian who's made most of her recent films in Hollywood, alongside several British actors and the odd American). Is this an Australian export? Or American exploitation of Australian resources?

National Cinemas

Clearly a book of this size cannot describe all the intricacies of the various National Cinemas – and some of the national film movements are discussed in the next chapter. I wish to concentrate on the Australian situation, but first a brief word on some others.

France has been through a number of periods of filmmaking, with the most significant period being the 1960s and the *Nouvelle Vague* (or New Wave). Many of the critics who had been working on the film journal *Cahiers Du Cinéma*, from which the *auteur* theory had emerged, began to make their own films, most notably Jean-Luc Godard, François Truffaut and Claude Chabrol. This generation of filmmakers was attempting to make a distinct break from the quality cinema of the previous generation by producing non-linear, morally ambiguous and stylistically complex movies. Shooting on the streets of Paris or in each other's apartments, and often casting friends and girlfriends in rôles, Godard brought a new sense of verisimilitude to film. As the decade progressed, the films became more political. The key film is probably *À Bout De Souffle* (1959) directed by Godard.

Spain's film history is dominated by its political landscape. Thanks to the dictatorial rule of General Francisco Franco from 1936 to 1975 there were strict limitations on what kinds of films were allowed to be made, and unlike many film-producing countries there were no film schools to train directors. In the years after Franco's death rules relaxed so much in Spain that it is now arguably the most liberal country in Europe. Pedro Almodóvar was ideally placed to take advantage of the new morality and made films featuring gay, lesbian and transvestite characters, portrayed the Church and the police as corrupt, offered rape and murder as ingredients, and wove in the culture of filmmaking. *La Ley Del Deseo* (1987; *Law Of Desire*) was his breakthrough film in terms of international audiences, and the follow-up, *Mujere Al Borde De Un Ataque De Nervios* (1988; *Women On The Verge Of A Nervous Breakdown*) was an even bigger success.

Japanese cinema is partially made in a different way from Western cinema, or at least it looks and feels very different from Classical Hollywood cinema since it doesn't fetishise continuity editing. At the same time, the cinema is held to be very representative of the Japanese character – and a recurring theme is the fallout of the first atom bombs to be used in war. Most of the movies that have come from Japan have effectively been placed within the art cinema category, given that the aesthetics are thought to be so different; *Hiroshima, Mon Amour* (1959) offers a co-production with Alain Resnais of the French New Wave, and a meditation on the consequences for the individual of the Second World War. The same anxieties can be seen in the various Godzilla movies and arguably in *Akira* (1988), the breakthrough anime, and Shinya

Tsukamoto's wonderful cyberpunk nightmare *Tetsuo* (1991). The four big names of Japanese cinema are Yasujiro Ozu (*Tokyo Monogatari, Tokyo Story*, 1952), Kenji Mizoguchi (*Saikaku Ichidai Onna, The Life Of Oharu*, 1952), Akira Kurosawa (*Shichinin No Samurai, Seven Samurai*, 1954) and Nagisa Oshima (*Ai No Corrida, In The Realm Of The Senses*, 1976).

Australian Cinema

Based on three films to emerge from Australia in the early 1990s, you would gain a queer view of the country: *Strictly Ballroom* (1992), *Muriel's Wedding* (1994), and *The Adventures Of Priscilla, Queen Of The Desert* (1994) all contained elements of camp and featured to varying degrees fluid sexualities, a fixation with Abba, an ugly duckling narrative and a degree of postmodern pastiche and parody. These three quirky films, alongside the Oscar-winning *Shine* (1996), were all international box-office successes. But there is a darker strand to 1990s Australian cinema: the racism of skinhead culture in Footscray in *Romper Stomper* (1992, financed by New Zealand), the much darker exploration of sexuality, drugs and being of immigrant stock in *Head On* (1997), the paranoid, jump-cut edited *Kiss Or Kill* (1997), and the true-crime adaptation *Chopper* (2000). Taken together, we have a national cinema which came to the healthiest point in its history, and then became the victim of its own success.

Australia is well placed to have a successful cinema – its English-language films can target both its old colonial power, Britain, and the United States – but the commercial success of Australian cinema has waxed and waned over the century. The first feature film was made in Australia – *Story Of The Kelly Gang* (1906) – and a reasonable number of films were shot in the middle of the silent era, but production became increasingly sporadic after the Second World War. *The Overlanders* (1946), *A Town Like Alice* (1956) and *On The Beach* (1959) all had Australian settings but weren't locally financed. Serious production in Australia didn't get under way until the 1970s with a so-called New Wave, and the early films of Peter Weir, Fred Schepisi, Bruce Beresford and the two George Millers.

This came about in part because of the establishment of the Australian Film Development Corporation (later the Australian Film Commission) in 1970 to finance the development of movies with government money; there were also funding bodies at the level of the individual state. This was supplemented by a series of tax rules which allowed investment to be written off, thus encouraging private funding of films. In the mid-1980s the tax rules changed, sending the industry into decline once more before the supplementing of the AFC with the Australian Film Finance Corporation in 1988. The AFFC has an annual grant to help finance films; other sources of revenue include various Australian television stations, most notably the Special Broadcasting Service (SBS), and production companies such as Southern Star. Many of the successful directors of the 1970s and early 1980s had been lured to America, for example Weir directing *Dead Poets Society* (1989) and *The Truman Show* (1998). In the mid-1980s only one film really broke through to international attention, *Crocodile Dundee* (1986), which took the eponymous hero from the Outback to New York and played with an Australian stereotype.

More recently, Australian cinema has been infiltrated by Hollywood studios, partially looking for more of the Independent-style quirky films which have broken through to an international market since the start of the 1990s, but also to exploit local technicians in much the same way as British technicians were used on block-buster films in the 1970s and 1980s. Fox (ultimately owned by Australian tycoon Rupert Murdoch) has studios in Sydney, the location for shooting much of *The Matrix* trilogy, and Warner Brothers teamed up with Village Roadshow to run a studio in Queensland.

Meanwhile, the films are distributed within Australia by Fox Columbia Tristar, Roadshow Film Distributors and United International Pictures, companies which have obvious links to American studios and distribu-tors. The chains of cinemas include Hoyts, Village Roadshow (aka Warner Village and Greater Union) and Reading, another American-backed corporation. There is also a thriving art circuit in the major cities.

So what is the Australian national character as depicted in Australian films? The Australian is an immi-grant or a descendent from an immigrant, predomi-nantly from waves of British colonisation over the last few centuries. Other European nationalities have moved to Australia, the Greek–Australian community being represented in *Death In Brunswick* (1990) and *Head On*, the latter also representing immigrants from Vietnam and Korea. There is the sense that Western culture has been imposed on the landscape and that the cities are not quite real (see *The Matrix*, filmed in Sydney). The various road movies which should offer self-discovery for their heroes do not offer the same sense of transformation. Two of the drag queens in *Priscilla* simply learn from their exposure to the Outback and King's Canyon that there's no place like home, and the landscape is so alien that it seems not to be comprehended.

The films feature several of the national stereotypes of the Australian (male): the bushman (*Crocodile Dundee*), the pioneer, the ANZAC soldier (see *Gallipoli*, 1981), the larrikin or city-based delinquent (Ari in *Head On*) and the ocker – the resourceful, cheerful yet boorish and chauvinist working man, who shades into the battler. Two films directed by Robert Sitch, *The Castle* (1997) and *The Dish* (2001), developed with the Working Dog team that had worked in television, show the battler at work. In the former the Kerrigan family face eviction from their idyllic home in order to allow an airport extension to be built. Dad Kerrigan reasons that this is his family's home, so it *can't* be demolished, and in the end he is successful, winning the (free) aid of a QC who is struck by Dad's common sense. The film can be criticised for its depiction of the Kerrigans – the ironic differences between the son's voice-over narration and what we see set the family up for ridicule. Further, the family's comparison of themselves to the dispossessed Aboriginals risks seeming racist, even though in the extended family there are Greek- and Lebanese-descended characters.

The Dish can seek comfort in nostalgia for a moment when Australia played a rôle on the world stage, the relaying of sounds and pictures back from the 1969 Moon landing. When the radio telescope temporarily loses Apollo 11 shortly before an official visit from the

American ambassador, the plucky members of the team imitate the astronaut and pretend nothing has gone wrong. It is the strait-laced NASA representative who is transformed during the course of the narrative and turns out to be a decent bloke after all, despite the framing narrative of Sam Neill (splendidly wearing a cardigan and smoking a pipe like a 50s dad) visiting the telescope as an old man. By then, Working Dog had a three-movie, first-look deal with Village Roadshow, a subsidiary of Warner Brothers, and rather knowingly used the American as the means of translating the film into a language which an international audience would be able to understand. The national character is laid bare for a world audience – to laugh at and admire.

Problems Of Discussing National Cinema

One of the problems of discussing national cinema is in defining what nation a particular film can be attributed to. The flow of international capital is only going to make this more and more complex, as non-American directors are funded by Hollywood and Hollywood follows tax shelters to new countries to film in, or searches for new technicians for the next generation of blockbusters.

The next problem is that for most of us our exposure to any nationality of cinema is going to be partial at best. Richard Lowenstein's adaptation of John Birmingham's flat-sharing memoirs *He Died With A Falafel In His Hand* (2000) set in Brisbane, Melbourne and Sydney, was shown at an Italian film festival and was the closing film of the Melbourne Film Festival in 2001. A wider release has not yet occurred. It could be that only the most successful films will be imported, or in the case of the art film, the artiest, so we don't see the whole spectrum from the most personal to the most commercial.

Finally, there is the problem of identifying national characteristics. Production and distribution details are comparatively easy to locate, but the nature of the characteristic content of a film is harder to pin down. Edward Said, in his book *Orientalism* (1978), identified a consistent set of values ascribed by the West to 'Orientals' – whether from Egypt or Arab countries, and by extension to Chinese, Japanese and other Far Eastern peoples. Even the terms Near, Middle and Far East are part of a Eurocentric bias that identifies the West as masculine, rational and modern and the East as feminine, irrational and old-fashioned. We risk imposing our own set of values and our own needs onto what we perceive in a nation. Equally, those within a particular culture may not best be placed to be objective about the specifics of their own national characteristics. It would be naïve to assume that a film straightforwardly represents a culture, or that an *auteur* is typical or definitive of a nation, but as more films are watched, so the detail can be filled in and inferred.

Chapter 12

Film Movements And Genres:
An Annotated Listing

This chapter is an attempt to define important move-ments and genres, some of which have not been discussed elsewhere in this book. Whilst this can't be complete (remember how many countries produce film, and may therefore have a new wave), it may at least be thought definitively incomplete. In each case I've suggested a film that's worth seeing to get the move-ment or genre in a nutshell.

Anime

Japanese cartoons, often drawn from comic books (manga) and featuring heroes with relatively western-ised features. The fast-paced narratives tend to draw on SCIENCE FICTION and often feature mutants with superpowers. *Akira* (1988).

Art Cinema

Term used to describe films, predominantly made outside of Hollywood, that attempt to act as personal expressions rather than simply aiming to make money, and which may be considered AVANT-GARDE. They

138

often feature non-linear narratives (if indeed they have narratives at all), open endings and ambiguous morality – in other words they reject CLASSICAL HOLLY-WOOD. These films often play in repertory art cinemas rather than multiplexes, although can occasionally turn into a hit. Arguably much of so-called INDEPEN-DENT cinema is art cinema. See also COUNTER CINEMA. *Der Himmel Über Berlin* (1987).

Avant-Garde

The 'advance guard', extremely experimental films which overlap with ART CINEMA. Whilst Art Cinema can often have financial backing from corporate sponsors, *avant-garde* films are more likely to be self-financed or funded by patrons. In many cases they might only be seen in art galleries or at film festivals. *Un Chien Andalou* (1928).

Blaxploitation

Films primarily aimed at black audiences in America in the early to mid-1970s, made by black directors, featuring black characters often battling against white characters. Heroes would include black private eyes or dealers trying to go straight, or strong female characters kicking butt. Whilst they do often tread an uneasy line in racial stereotypes, they offered blacks a much wider range of rôles than before. See also NEW JACK CINEMA. *Shaft* (1971).

B-Movie

Product of the studio system from the 1930s and 1940s, a movie churned out quickly to form the second feature alongside a more prestigious or A-Movie. In retrospect many of these films are more interesting than the A-Movies. *Detour* (1945).

Body Horror

Subgenre of horror which focuses upon the invasion of the body or the body betraying its 'owner' in some way, often by playing host to some virus or parasite. See in fact pretty well all of David Cronenberg's output. *Videodrome* (1982).

British New Wave

Movement within British cinema of the 1950s and 1960s, an expansion on the Angry Young Man school of theatre, filming many of those plays. Typical subjects were working-class male life, although sexuality and the rôle of women were also considered. It was influenced by FREE BRITISH CINEMA and KITCHEN SINK DRAMA. Central directors included Tony Richardson and Karel Reisz, and it made stars of Albert Finney and Michael Caine. *A Taste Of Honey* (1961).

Buddy Movie

Movie featuring two male friends, who often bicker, but help each other through various troubles. Women are sidelined, and there may often be a homosexual subtext. Often the buddies may be of separate races, or even species. The buddy movie can overlap with other genres – DETECTIVE, ROAD MOVIE, SCIENCE FICTION, WAR and so on. Female buddy movies exist but are rare – see *Thelma And Louise* (1991), if you must. *Thunderbolt And Lightfoot* (1974).

Chick Flick

Faintly derogatory term derived from *Sleepless In Seattle* (1993) to refer to any movie more likely to appeal to a woman than a man, often featuring strong female characters in MELODRAMA plots. In the late 1990s cinemas started screening chick flicks to coincide with major sporting events, to try to tap into a female audience. *An Affair To Remember* (1957).

Classical Hollywood Cinema

The period of film history dominated by the major Hollywood studios, perhaps marked by the Hays Code from 1934 to 1968, although the anti-trust actions successfully brought against the studios by exhibitors in 1948 marked the start of the decline. Stylistically these films were marked by continuity editing and a sense of realism, at least in the creation of on-screen space. The history of this cinema is the history of genres (and vice versa). The period after the 1960s is known as post-Classical Hollywood. *Casablanca* (1942).

Comedy

Any film designed to make an audience laugh – a genre which can be subdivided into GROSS-OUT COMEDY, ROMANTIC COMEDY, SLAPSTICK COMEDY and so on. *A Night At The Opera* (1935).

Counter Cinema

Another phrase for ART CINEMA, coined by Peter Wollen, and to be contrasted with CLASSICAL HOLLYWOOD. These films are open to multiple interpretations, resist having easy identification with characters, and don't aim to give easy pleasures. *Vent D'Est* (1970).

Detective/Private Eye

Interrelated genres involving the investigation of crimes, usually murders. The private eye is usually on the edge of legality and isolated from the rest of society. Clearly this can – though doesn't have to – overlap with *FILM NOIR*. Equally, characters who are policemen tend to be mavericks, playing by their own rules. *The Big Sleep* (1946).

Dogme 95

A group of filmmakers, centred on Lars Van Trier, drew up a manifesto which was a vow of chastity, to avoid the falsity of studio equipment and sets, to use natural sound and lighting, to film where events happened rather than staging things, and to avoid MELODRA-

MATIC narratives. Films which observe the strictures (although some do cheat) are awarded a Dogme certificate and now have been made in Denmark, America, Spain, Belgium, Sweden, Argentina and elsewhere. It's not clear whether the original manifesto was serious or a joke. *Idioterne* (1998).

Dziga-Vertov Group

Group of politically committed Marxist filmmakers which emerged out of the FRENCH NEW WAVE – centring on Jean-Luc Godard and Jean-Pierre Gorin. The group started in May 1968 and disbanded in 1973, taking its name from the Soviet filmmaker best known for *Man With A Movie Camera* (1929). *Letter To Jane* (1972).

Ealing Comedies

Films made in the 1940s and 1950s by Ealing Studios featuring groups of people battling against authority, often on the edge of or the wrong side of the law – whether maintaining the independence of Pimlico, stealing whisky from a wreck, or attempting to sneak stolen money past a dear old lady. Whilst audiences were often asked to sympathise with thieves and murderers, justice was usually seen to be done. *Kind Hearts And Coronets* (1949).

Epic

Large-budget films telling big, important stories, often over several hours, featuring casts of thousands and much spectacle. Whilst epics on Biblical topics or American history date back to the First World War, the form really came into its own in the 1950s as cinemascope and Technicolor became weapons in cinema's fight against competition from television – although flops like *Cleopatra* (1963) were costly failures in this battle. *Gladiator* (2000).

Fantasy

A wide-ranging genre which features events that cannot happen in the real world, whether magic, dragons or flying. Fantasy can involve such elements breaking into the real world, an entry into a fantasy world from the real (often ambiguous as to whether it is actual or just a dream), or be entirely set in the fantasy world. Often dismissed as being just for kids, or being escapist, fantasy offers scope for commentary on the real world and relationships from an unusual angle. *The Lord Of The Rings* (2001, 2002, 2003).

Film Noir

Film equivalent of the *noir* fiction of the 1930s, often featuring DETECTIVE/PRIVATE EYE protagonists in MELODRAMAs in amoral universes: double-crosses, blackmail, bribery and murders, as well as a dangerous female character or *femme fatale*. The *mise en scène* is often dark and shadowed, with unusual camera angles, reminiscent of GERMAN EXPRESSIONISM. French critics coined the term in 1946 to refer to a genre which flourished between about 1940 and 1960. *NEO NOIR* draws upon much of its imagery, themes and narratives. *Double Indemnity* (1944).

Free British Cinema

Term coined by director Lindsay Anderson in 1956 covering the personal ART CINEMA shorts and documentaries about everyday working-class life he compiled for the British National Film Theatre. The directors were from a number of countries, but prepared the way for the BRITISH NEW WAVE. *Every Day Except Christmas* (1957).

French New Wave

Movement within French cinema of the late 1950s and 1960s, including several critics from the *Cahiers Du Cinéma*: Jean-Luc Godard, Claude Chabrol, Eric Rohmer and François Truffaut. Their output was mostly ART CINEMA or COUNTER CINEMA, featuring real locations, non-professional actors, moral ambiguity and open endings. As the 1960s wore on some of the directors became more politicised, and Godard set up the DZIGA-VERTOV GROUP. *Week-End* (1967).

Gangsters

Like the WESTERN, a genre which mythifies a period in American history, in particular the Prohibition era. A central part of Warner Brothers output in the 1930s, the films enabled producers to have their cake and eat it: they could provide violent thrills for their audiences whilst claiming they were calling for the government to crack down. *The Godfather* (1971) gave the genre a new lease of life, whilst Martin Scorsese portrayed an image of the more contemporary gangster in *Goodfellas* (1990) and *Casino* (1995). In some ways, they have shaded into *NEO NOIR*. After the Second World War British cinema began mimicking gangster films, with some success, developing a sense of realism that was to feed into the BRITISH NEW WAVE; British cinema revitalised the genre in the last decade although the mockney rapidly grew thin. *Once Upon A Time In America* (1983).

German Expressionism

Movement in German cinema which flourished from after the First World War to the early 1930s, characterised by oblique camera angles and use of light and shadows rather than realism. The narratives often drew on folk tales or gothic HORROR, and explored psychological states. The movement was a direct influence upon Alfred Hitchcock who worked in Germany in the mid-1920s. Some of its practitioners emigrated to America where they influenced first the Universal horrors of the 1930s and then the look of *FILM NOIR*. *Das Kabinett Des Dr Caligari* (1919).

Gross-Out Comedy

Branch of COMEDY characterised by obsession with bodily functions, genitalia, food, excreta, sex, and a general lack of taste. *There's Something About Mary* (1998).

Horror

Genre of film designed to shock or frighten, usually thought of as occurring in cycles: supernatural tales in GERMAN EXPRESSIONISM, the cycle of Universal horrors in the 1930s, the monster movies of the 1950s, the Hammer movies from the 1950s to the 1970s, the SLASHER MOVIEs from the 1970s onwards and so on; see also BODY HORROR. *Bride Of Frankenstein* (1935).

Independent

Usually low-budget movies, made out of studio control, often personal expressions akin to ART CINEMA. Given the limited amount of independent distribution, so-called independent films are often completed by studio money and distributed with their other products. Some studios have divisions dedicated to making quasi-Independent product or manufacturing sleeper hits. Term only really has meaning in relation to American films of the 1980s and 1990s. *Clerks* (1994).

Kitchen Sink Drama

Kind of realism typical of the BRITISH NEW WAVE – featuring working-class, usually northern, everyday life. *Saturday Night And Sunday Morning* (1960).

Literary Adaptation

Most films are based on earlier narratives, although it is probably a truism to say that the better the book, the poorer the film. Adaptations come in three broad kinds: faithful translations from page to screen (see much of Merchant Ivory's output), unfaithful adaptations where things are changed for no real reason, and adaptations that offer a commentary on the original material (see *Mansfield Park* (1999)). *The Maltese Falcon* (1941).

Melodrama

Genre, usually thought of as being aimed at women, and based around events that threaten the continuance of a family – a divorce, a death, an unwanted pregnancy, bankruptcy. A female character is usually central to the drama. *Imitation Of Life* (1959).

Musical

Genre of films which have characters suddenly bursting into song for no readily explicable reason and not getting locked up for it. Some people like this kind of thing. The narratives are often little more than hooks for song and dance routines – the Marx Brothers regularly had them inserted into their movies alongside a dull ROMANCE plot. MGM was the studio most associated with the musical. *The Sound Of Music* (1965).

Neo Noir

Updating of the *FILM NOIR*, sometimes remaking old *noir* narratives, and including *femmes fatales*, double-crossing and triple-crossing, physical violence, extreme language and night shoots. Downbeat endings were unusually prevalent for Hollywood films. *LA Confidential* (1997).

Neo-Realism

A movement in Italian cinema from the early 1940s to the early 1950s, centring on Vittorio De Sica, Roberto Rossellini and Luchino Visconti in reaction against the limitation of expression then in place. Characterised by a striving for realism, using location rather than studios, dealing with social issues and having authentic, often overlapping, dialogue. It was an influence of the aesthetics of the FRENCH and BRITISH NEW WAVEs. *Roma, Città Aperta* (1945).

New German Cinema

Flowering of German cinema in the 1960s and 1970s, centring on Rainer Werner Fassbinder, but also including Wim Wenders and Werner Herzog, dealing with social issues in contemporary Germany. A collective approach to distribution ensured export of their film, especially on the ART FILM circuit. *Jeder Für Sich Und Gotte Gegen Alle* (1974).

New Jack Cinema

Name given to films produced on black themes in the 1990s, with a harder edge than the BLAXPLOITA-TION of 20 years earlier. Primarily they dealt with life in the ghetto and the ways out of there – through the army, through education, by going to prison and by leaving in a coffin. *New Jack City* (1991).

New Queer Cinema

Marketing label given to the output of gay and lesbian directors during the early 1990s who were successful on the festival circuit. Rather than featuring gays as losers or psychopaths, they featured gays as murderers and sociopaths, getting on with their lives in the era of AIDS but not having a problem with their sexuality. Derek Jarman was a kind of godmother to the movement, although many of the directors owed more to the aesthetics of Scorsese and Tarantino. In a sense the movement became absorbed into the mainstream as gay characters appeared in all sorts of movies, including ROMANTIC COMEDIES. *Swoon* (1991).

Road Movie

Any movie featuring characters travelling, whether by car, motorbike or lavender bus. Usually on the course of their journey and the experiences along the way, the characters learn about who they really are. The films tend to be episodic. *Easy Rider* (1969).

Romance

Any film where the central narrative is two characters falling in love and overcoming the obstacles in their way. Usually thought of as a woman's genre. *Before Sunrise* (1995).

Romantic Comedy

Combination of the romance plot and the comedy, in which two people, who begin by disliking each other, eventually fall in love. As traditional barriers like class and paternal disapproval have faded, new obstacles have been found – such as the characters' sexuality and being on different coasts. These days it is all too likely that one of the two actors will be making this film in a break from their sitcom. *Sleepless In Seattle* (1993).

Science Fiction

A genre of film which often overlaps with HORROR; usually the narrative is centred on the impact of science or technology, although increasingly this is just an excuse to hang a series of set-piece special effects together and scientific rigour can go hang as we see light travel through a vacuum, and hear those explosions in space. *Alien* (1979).

Screwball Comedy

Complexly plotted comedies, usually featuring an outrageous, strong female who dazzles a rather shy male, and gets him into a series of scrapes as they fall in love. The dialogue is rapid and sometimes overlapping. *Bringing Up Baby* (1938).

Slapstick Comedy

Branch of COMEDY typified by pratfalls, custard pies, chases, buckets of water and lots of falling over – in other words a typical Friday night after the pub. In the silent era and immediately afterwards these were churned out in their hundreds, often featuring a recurring character or characters. Buster Keaton and Harry Lloyd were masters of physical comedy, whereas Charles Chaplin is too sentimental for some tastes. *The Music Box* (1932).

Slasher Movies

Subgenre of HORROR movies featuring an apparently unstoppable killer murdering young people one by one until he (or she) faces a final girl. See chapter on Genres for more details. *Halloween* (1978).

Soviet Montage

From the typical editing technique of Sergei Eisenstein, by extension to a school of filmmakers and film theorists of the 1920s. The filmmakers' concern with social and political issues led them to cerate a cinema where people were moved emotionally and manipulated intellectually. *Battleship Potemkin* (1925).

Spaghetti Westerns

Subgenre of WESTERNs, made in the 1960s and 1970s, shot by Italian directors in Spain. Morality is up for grabs, people lie and cheat and get killed, and the iconography of the more straightforward Western is parodied or fetishised. *Once Upon A Time In The West* (1968).

Teen Movie

Any movie made from the 1950s to the present day, aimed at a youth demographic. Initially they featured the horrors of growing up in middle-class Britain and America, juggling dilemmas of school work, young love and being cool, but increasingly this is shot in a music video style and fused with the retelling of a familiar narrative from Shakespeare, Jane Austen, Charles Dickens and others. Many SLASHER HORROR films are teen pics. *10 Things I Hate About You* (1999).

Third Cinema

Term coined in 1969 by Solanas and Getino to describe films made within the 'Third World' – especially within Latin America – which were often oppositional to their nation's dominant ideology. First Cinema is Hollywood and Second is European cinema. The term risks creating a pecking order of film and rather homogenises a vast array of World Cinema. *Orfeu Negro* (1959).

Western

Genre which is almost as old as film itself, mythifying the Wild West of nineteenth-century America, and featuring a cowboy either struggling to make a living in a hostile landscape, or confronting (or often being confronted by) native Americans. Westerns were made from the silent period through to the 1960s, but have been rarer since, perhaps due to the ideological unsoundness of the portrayals of Indians. On the other hand, the Hollywood output became eclipsed by SPAGHETTI WESTERNS. The iconography of the films – Monument Valley, six-guns, shoot-outs, horse-manship – is immediately recognisable, and has been endlessly parodied as well as transferred into SCIENCE FICTION. *Stagecoach* (1939).

References

Select Bibliography

Some of the books and articles I've used in writing this book, and pointers for further reading, with occasional annotations.

Althusser, Louis, 1984. *Essays on Ideology*. London:Verso.

Andrew, J. Dudley, 1976. *The Major Film Theories: An Introduction*. Oxford: Oxford University Press. [Useful overview of theorists of film]

Arnheim, Rudolf, 1957. *Film as Art*. Berkeley and Los Angeles: University of California Press.

Banker, Ashok, 2001, *Bollywood*. Harpenden: Pocket Essentials.

Barthes, Roland, 1993. *Mythologies*. London: Vintage. [Classic structuralist analysis of pop culture, including films, with a useful section on mythology]

Bordwell, David and Thompson, Kristin, 1990. *Film Art: An Introduction*. New York: McGraw-Hill. [Study of formal elements of film – but increasingly overpriced]

Braudy, Leo and Cohen, Marshall, eds., 1999. *Film Theory And Criticism: Introductory Readings*. Oxford: Oxford University Press. [A good place to dip in for actual film theory – authorship, spectatorship, genre theory and much more – Münsterberg, Arnheim, Pudovkin, Eisenstein, Sarris, Wollen, Mulvey, Altman, Narboni and much more. Essential.]

Butler, Andrew M. and Bob Ford, 2003. *Postmodernism*. Harpenden: Pocket Essentials.

Clover, Carol J., 1993. *Men, Women And Chainsaws: Gender In The Modern Horror Film*. London: BFI. [Useful and stimulating study of horror]

Cohan, Steven and Hark, Ina Rae, eds., 1997. *The Road Movie Book*. London and New York: Routledge.

Cook, Pam, 1985. *The Cinema Book*. London: BFI.

Cooke, Paul, 2002. *German Expressionist Film*. Harpenden: Pocket Essentials.

Craven, Ian, ed., 2000. *Australian Cinema In The 1990s*. Ilford and Portland: Frank Cass.

Duncan, Paul, 2000, *Film Noir*. Harpenden: Pocket Essentials.

Dyer, Richard, 1998 [2nd ed.]. *Stars*. London: BFI.

Fitzgerald, Martin, 2000. *Hong Kong's Heroic Bloodshed*. Harpenden: Pocket Essentials.

Frayling, Christopher, 1998. *Spaghetti Westerns: Cowboys And Europeans From Karl May To Sergio Leone*. London: Tauris.

Gramsci, Antonio, 1985. *Selections from Cultural Writings*. London: Lawrence and Wishart.

Hill, John and Gibson, Pamela Church, eds., 1998. *The Oxford Guide To Film Studies*. Oxford: Oxford University Press. [Contains short essays on various aspects of Hollywood, European and World Cinema; a little difficult to navigate]

Hollows, Joanne and Jancovich, Mark, eds., 1995. *Approaches To Popular Film*. Manchester: Manchester University Press.

Hughes, Howard, 2001, *Spaghetti Westerns*. Harpenden: Pocket Essentials.

Jameson, Fredric, 1991. *Postmodernism or, The Cultural Logic of Late Capitalism*. London and New York:Verso.

Kaplan, E. Ann, ed., 1980. *Women And Film Noir*. London: BFI.

Koven, Mikel J., 2001. *Blaxploitation Films*. Harpenden: Pocket Essentials.

Kracauer, Siegfried, 1947. *From Caligari To Hitler: A Psychological History Of The German Film*. Princeton: Princeton University Press.

Kuhn, Annette, ed., 1990. *Alien Zone: Cultural Theory And Contemporary Science Fiction Cinema*. New York and London:Verso.

Münsterberg, Hugo, 2002. *Hugo Münsterberg on Film: The Photoplay: A Psychological Study and Other Writings*. New York and London: Routledge.

Neale, Stephen, 1980. *Genre*. London: BFI. [Key thinking on genre]

Neale, Steve and Smith, Murray, eds., 1998. *Contemporary Hollywood Cinema*. London and New York: Routledge.

Odell, Colin and Le Blanc, Michelle, 2001. *Horror Films*. Harpenden: Pocket Essentials.

Odell, Colin and Le Blanc, Michelle, 2001. *John Carpenter*. Harpenden: Pocket Essentials.

Odell, Colin and Le Blanc, Michelle, 2000. *Vampire Films*. Harpenden: Pocket Essentials.

Perkins, V. F., 1972. *Film As Film*. Harmondsworth, Middlesex: Pelican. [Decent common sense approach to film]

Pierson, John, 1997. *Spike, Mike, Slackers And Dykes: A Guided Tour Across A Decade Of American Independent*

Cinema. New York: Miramax/Hyperion.

Pudovkin, Vsevolod, 1958. *Film Technique and Film Acting*.

Rich, B. Ruby, 1992. 'New Queer Cinema.' *Sight & Sound* 2:5, 31–34.

Russell, Jamie, 2002. *Vietnam War Movies*. Harpenden: Pocket Essentials.

Russo, Vito, 1987. *The Celluloid Closet*. New York: Harper and Row. [Useful history of gay cinema]

Said, Edward, 1978. *Orientalism: Western Conceptions Of The Orient*. Harmondsworth, Middlesex: Penguin.

Stacey, Jackie, 1994. *Stargazing*. London: Routledge.

Truffaut, François, 1954. 'A Certain Tendency In French Cinema.' In Bill Nichols, ed., 1985. *Movies And Methods Volume II*. Berkeley: University of California Press.

Whitehead, Mark, 2000. *Slasher Movies*. Harpenden: Pocket Essentials.

Wiegand, Chris, 2001. *French New Wave*. Harpenden: Pocket Essentials.

Wollen, Peter, 1972. *Signs And Meaning In The Cinema*. London: Secker and Warburg/BFI.

Wood, Robin, 1986. *Hollywood From Vietnam To Reagan*. New York: Columbia University Press.

Wood, Robin, 1992. *Hitchcock's Films Revisited*. London and Boston: Faber & Faber.

Websites

Of course, there are far too many of these to list, but the most useful is www.imdb.com, the Internet Movie Database, first port of call for film data and information. For a longer listing, as well as a filmography and updates

to this volume, see homepages.enterprise.net/ambutler/
pe/film.htm.

Film Studies

A useful site for film, media and cultural studies –
www.aber.ac.uk/media/Functions/mcs.html

Organisations

American Film Institute – www.afi.com

British Film Institute – access to library catalogue,
details of *Sight And Sound*, some reviews, some special
articles, National Film Theatre schedules – www.bfi.
org.uk

British Board of Film Classification – www.bbfc.org

Gossip

Ain't It Cool News – www.aint-it-cool-news.com

Reviews

Roger Ebert – www.suntimes.com/index/ebcrt

Film.Com – archives of reviews, news and trailers –
www.film.com

Movie review query engine – www.mrqe.com

Studios

Buena Vista – www.buenavista.com/
Miramax – www.miramax.com
MGM – www.mgm.com
Paramount – www.paramount.com
Twentieth-Century Fox – www.foxmovies.com
Universal Studios – www.universalstudios.com
Warner Brothers – www.warnerbros.com